PUSHED INTO POSITION

PROCESSED FOR KINGDOM PURPOSE

A Story with an Amazing Twist

Karen Bolden

Foreword By Dr Pearl Kupe

ISBN 978-1-64299-585-5 (paperback)
ISBN 978-1-64299-586-2 (digital)

Christian Faith Publishing, Inc.
832 Park Avenue
Meadville, PA 16335
www.christianfaithpublishing.com

Photo by Charnika Jett
chary-jay.com

Printed in the United States of America

To My Lord and Savior Jesus Christ

To my husband, Shawn Bolden, whom I love dearly and who has shown me that God heals all wounds and restores us beyond what we could ever dream or imagine.

To my beautiful, heaven-sent young men Timothy, Timitheus, and TiKyran who have been my inspiration.

In Memory

To my daddy: I will never forget how he believed in me and all that I did. He was a great inspiration to me. I will always hold the memories of my precious daddy in my heart. I will meet him again.

To my God-dad, Deacon Jimmie: I will always remember how he stepped in and became a dad to me and loved me and the boys like we were from his loins. I will meet him again.

To my Grandmother Ella: I appreciate the many years of wisdom and love that she poured into me. I will meet her again.

Special Thanks

To my wonderful mother who have been my rock,
my friend, my support. To my spiritual father Bishop
Thomas L. Johnson - thank you for all that you poured
into me that contributed to who I've become today.
To my cousin Tamica and sisters who have loved me, cried with me,
understood me, prayed with and for me, and stood by my side.
I appreciate and love you dearly.
Kingdom Blessings!

CONTENTS

FOREWORD

This amazing book, *Pushed into Position* is a moving account of Karen Bolden's "real life" and personal testimony of how God took a broken life and put it together for His good and for Kingdom benefit!

It tells a story of a young girl who went through various traumatizing experiences, including rejection and abuse and this abuse continued in her life as a young woman. These experiences did not BREAK her but instead BUILT her and brought her and her family to a place where they could be used as instruments in the hands of the Master to BUILD His Kingdom. This is a moving and authentic testimony of Salvation, Deliverance & Healing that will provoke the salvation and healing of many hurting people.

This book will not only open the eyes of many to know that they are NOT alone, but also to the TRUTH that there is a HELP that they can connect to and His name is JESUS. God has taken the ashes of Karen's former life and created a great inner and outer

BEAUTY out of them. The beauty that God has brought out in you, woman of God, will provoke a similar beauty in many others. May this book bring inner healing and peace to all who read it and may what the Lord has done for you be experienced by many others.

—Dr. Pearl Kupe, Attorney, International
consultant & International President,
Global Forum for Women Entrepreneurs

INTRODUCTION

The Lord blessed me to launch my first book in 2012. I started writing originally in 2009, and of course, life's circumstances and distractions got in the way, so I put the writing on hold. However, one Sunday morning, April of 2011, I was in service and the guest minister's message was, "This is the year of unstoppable progress."

It is very important that, as people of God, we position ourselves to hear and receive the things that the Lord has set for us. Almost every word he spoke served as confirmation of the word that God had given me to speak at a conference in Virginia Beach, Virginia, a month earlier. I knew, without a shadow of doubt, I was in a place where I needed to be attentive and listen to the voice of God because I was getting divine instruction. Within four months, I had completed *Pushed into Position*. Little did I know that shortly after my book was released, my world would look nothing like it did and would be changed entirely. The enemy tried to use what he thought would destroy me, but God took what the enemy thought would destroy me to *push me into kingdom purpose according to His* determinate counsel: that in which He predestined for my life before the foundation of the world.

> ***"Before I formed thee in the belly I knew thee; and before thou camest forth out of the womb I sanctified thee, and I ordained thee a prophet unto the nations" (Jeremiah 1:5).***

This book serves as a testament (tangible proof) that despite life's heartaches, disappointments, and roadblocks, in Christ, you can walk away victorious and that we have the power to take dominion over every principality and powers of darkness in the earth realm through the power given to us through the Holy Spirit. I have been victorious over every plot of the enemy; not even sexual abuse, rape, physical abuse, divorced parents as a teenager, rejection, anger, rebelliousness, unforgiveness, infidelity, and divorce could stop me from my destiny. This is a story of the miracle of true love of Christ, God's amazing grace, and so much more. I thank God for His grace and mercy. I thank Him for the gift of faith and salvation.

> ***"For by grace are ye saved through faith; and that not of yourselves: it is the gift of God: Not of works, lest any man should boast. For we are his workmanship, created in Christ Jesus unto good works, which God hath before ordained that we should walk in them" (Ephesians 2:8–10).***

Today, I serve in multifaceted areas of ministry in the Kingdom of our Lord and Savior Jesus Christ with a heart and mind to carry out and fulfill the mandate that God has place upon my life.

> ***"But he that knew not, and did commit things worthy of stripes, shall be beaten with few stripes. For unto whomsoever much is given, of him shall be much required: and to whom men have committed much, of him they will ask the more" (Luke 12:48).***

God turned my life around and allowed my tests, trials, tribulation, circumstances, and situations to push me into the position of His Kingdom dominion and purpose. We don't have to allow life to overtake us. We must learn to overtake life. We are to be positioned to dominate the earth realm in Kingdom authority through the keys given to us by our Lord and Savior Jesus Christ. I pray that this book encourages and inspires you to do great things in God. I share my deep personal experiences and encounters with you, not for pity but that you, your loved one, or someone you may know can find themselves in my story and know that true deliverance can be our portion and that you do not have to remain in a position beneath what God have ordained. May you encounter a life-changing experience as I walk you through my life and share my story with you. Kingdom Blessings!

CHAPTER 1

Illegally Accessed

I was born and raised in the city of Detroit in a well-respected middle-class family. My father was a Detroit police officer. My mother was a housewife, but she worked as needed. They were good parents. They always provided a good home for us, supplied all our needs, and made us feel loved. We took family vacations and had many family gatherings. Our house was the house that everyone gathered at for family functions. My dad was a fun-loving, free-spirited type of guy, and my mom was just a great mom. They believed in God but were not faithful Christians. As a matter of fact, I don't ever recall my dad going to church, but my mom would occasionally go or send us with others. So I knew of God but did not know God.

However, unbeknownst to them, they would put their trust in the hands of someone who betrayed it. By the age of six, I had been molested several times and finally raped by a family member. This young man was someone who everyone loved. He was our babysitter. My parents had no idea what was happening to me because it was something they probably could have never imagined.

I remember it like it was yesterday. He babysat my brother, sister, and me. He started by fondling me on occasion, then it became more frequent. He fondled me as well as himself quite often. One evening, he made me get in the bed with him and taunted me all night. He fondled me for hours until he finally went all the way. The pain was horrid. The morning after it happened, I remember being in the bathroom crying. I was in a lot of pain. My uncle knocked on the door and asked me what was wrong and if I was okay. I wanted so badly to tell him what happened to me that night, but fear had set in. So, I told him that my stomach was hurting. In actuality, I was hurting emotionally and physically from the trauma that took place the night before.

Many children are afraid to tell someone about their abuse. Once they have been violated, "illegally accessed," this opens the door to so many different emotions and spirits such as fear, rejection, lust, etc., and these spirits are associated with so many issues that oftentimes shows up in adulthood if they are not addressed properly through counseling and spiritual interventions. It is extremely important that as parents, you talk to your children about sexual abuse. Teach them that there is a good touch and a bad touch. Teach them to tell if someone touches them in the wrong way. Don't assume that it can't happen to your child. This type of abuse happens more often than you think and can lead to years of emotional and behavior problems if it is not addressed early on. Parents, look for changes in behavior. It is so important that, as parents, we pay close attention to our children and their behaviors. Have open communication with your children concerning child predators. I can't stress it enough because this crime is so prevalent. Unfortunately, television and social media display obscene images on their shows and sites that have desensitized many to this growing and prevalent crime.

Don't think that if your child has been abused, it's your fault. It's not. It is the abuser's fault. Many parents feel that if they just ignore it or deny it, then the problem will go away—that it never existed. This is so far from the truth. It will only make matters worse. The child needs to know that he or she can trust you to address and handle the matter. Doing nothing will only send them into a shell, and they will eventually become a ticking time bomb.

I suppressed the pain for years, as many hurting victims do. God's grace was upon me as a child because most children go through life feeling as though what happened to them was their fault, feeling shame and guilt, but I knew in my heart that it wasn't my fault. If you have been abused, it is not your fault. Nothing that you say or do warrants this type of behavior. Your abuser needs help, and the only way he or she can get that help is for you to expose them. He or she have, at one point in their life, opened the door for demonic spirits to access them.

I know that my story is not unique. Millions of children suffer from sexual abuse. Sexual abuse was even prevalent in biblical days. King David's son, Amnon, raped his own sister. Sexual abusers have an unnatural obsession for their victims. It is a perverted (corrupt or immorally wrong) spirit.

> ***And when she had brought them unto him to eat, he took hold of her, and said unto her, Come lie with me, my sister. And she answered him, Nay, my brother, do not force me; for no such thing ought to be done in Israel: do not thou this folly. And I, whither shall I cause my shame to go? And as for thee, thou shalt be as one of the fools in Israel. Now therefore, I pray thee, speak unto the king; for he will not withhold me from thee. Howbeit he would not hearken unto her voice; but being stronger than she, forced her, and lay with her. (2 Samuel 13:11–14)***

Tamar was once a royal princess that was supposed to have an arranged marriage to a royal prince. However, this never happened because of the disgrace of her rape. She was condemned to live as an unmarried, childless woman. Offenders don't care how they can negatively affect and scar their victims for the rest of their lives. These types of acts are more prevalent now than ever. Only God has the ability to totally deliver us from the hurts and wounds of our past abuse. We must seek Him in a place beyond our emotions and pain. We must seek Him and experience His presence. Intimacy with God is a place where our spirit man connects with God. He gives us spiritual restoration, healing, and deliverance in a way that we would never imagine possible. We achieve this by praying, fasting, reading the Word of God, and getting spiritual guidance and counsel from spiritual leaders and mentors. It sometimes takes outside counseling as well. Please know that it is definitely okay to do that.

As a victim of abuse, know that you do not have to accept the emotional roller coaster that comes with the abuse. You have the power and the authority to take your life back. You don't have to accept a life of pain and misery. The devil is a liar! Get up from that place, and take your life back. *We can do all things through Christ who strengthens us* (see Philippians 4:13).

I'm reminded of a woman in the Bible known as the Shunammite woman. She was a blessing to the Prophet Elisha, and because she was a blessing to him, he asked her what could he do for her. She did not want anything, but Elisha insisted. He asked his servant and he told him that she did not have a child, and her husband was old. He told her that God would allow her to conceive a child, and it came to pass. However, the Bible says that, one day, the child went out to work in the field and fell ill and died.

> ***And he said unto his father, My head, my head. And he said to a lad, Carry him to his mother. And when he had taken him, and brought him to his mother, he sat on her knees till noon, and then died. And she went up, and laid him on the bed of the man of God, and shut the door upon him, and went out. And she called unto her husband, and said, Send me, I pray thee, one of the young men, and one of the asses, that I may run to the man of God, and come again. 3And he said, Wherefore wilt thou go to him today? It is neither new moon, nor Sabbath. And she said, It shall be well. Then she saddled an ass, and said to***

her servant, Drive, and go forward; slack not thy riding for me, except I bid thee. So she went and came unto the man of God to Mount Carmel. And it came to pass, when the man of God saw her afar off, that he said to Gehazi his servant, Behold, yonder is that Shunammite: Run now, I pray thee, to meet her, and say unto her, Is it well with thee? Is it well with thy husband? Is it well with the child? And she answered, It is well.

And when Elisha was come into the house, behold, the child was dead, and laid upon his bed. He went in therefore, and shut the door upon them twain, and prayed unto the LORD. And he went up, and lay upon the child, and put his mouth upon his mouth, and his eyes upon his eyes, and his hands upon his hands: and he stretched himself upon the child; and the flesh of the child waxed warm. Then he returned, and walked in the house to and fro; and went up, and stretched himself upon him: and the child sneezed seven times, and the child opened his eyes. (2 Kings 4:19–26, 32–35, KJV)

The Shunammite woman was determined not to allow this tragedy to cause her to give up and lose faith in God. So she decided to get up from where she was and pursue the prophet of God. She was looking for nothing short of a miracle. She believed that if she could just bring Elisha back to the child, God would use him to heal the child and bring him back to life, and that's exactly what happened. Her faith is what moved God. Your faith can move God in such a way that He will do even the very thing that does not make sense or that seems at first impossible. She told her driver to drive and go forth. She told him not to stop until he got to the man of God. Sometimes, we have to move forward and not stop until we become free in our heart, soul, and mind. I encourage you to drive and go forward in your life in spite of life's misfortunes. God is a healer and a deliverer. If you trust and believe in Him, He will see you through.

Sometimes it takes bulldog tenacity. I'm talking about the tenacity that causes you to hold firm to and be persistent about your deliverance. You have to make a determination that the enemy cannot and will not have your life by being and remaining focused on your liberty in body, mind, and spirit!

CHAPTER 2

Life-Changing Experience

My life changed forever when I was fifteen. One day, my brother and I were driving up the street. We ran into our father with another woman. This woman happened to be a friend of the family. My sister came home on another occasion and told me that she saw him at the other woman's house. She was going over to my uncle's girlfriend's house, who happened to be this other woman's sister. She stayed downstairs from her in a two-family flat. She said that when she went upstairs, the door was open, the blinds were up, and he was sitting on the couch. However, when she came back down, the door was closed, and the blinds were down.

This was devastating news. I didn't know how to handle the emotions that came along with this. I became very angry and felt insecure, but I just suppressed it. I watched my dad start arguments with my mom on her off days so he would have an excuse to leave the house. On the days she worked, a half hour after she left for work, he would get up, jump in the shower, put on nice clothes and some cologne and leave. He would come back a half hour before she came in, jump on the couch, light up a cigarette, and act as if he had been home all day with us. The tension was so high in the house. I believe he knew that we knew what was going on. It was a miserable situation.

One night, I was home with my brother and sister. I had been drinking. My brother's girlfriend had brought over alcohol. I was torn-up drunk. I received a phone call from my cousin who worked with me at a local restaurant. She told me that we didn't get a ten-cent raise because although we were excellent employees, we talked too much on the job. This little piece of information was like the pin that burst the balloon. I lost it! I had a huge anxiety attack. This was a very devastating time for me as a teenager. I was in my eleventh grade, in high school. I was supposed to be happy and enjoying life. Here I was, depressed and devastated. I didn't know how to handle the emotions that came along with this. I couldn't breathe. I was hollering, screaming, and just going plain crazy.

My brother ran across the street to a neighbor's house, and my sister didn't know what to do. My dad was gone, as usual, and my mom was at work. The irony of all this was that my mom was not supposed to get off work until one thirty in the morning, but she came home about ten minutes after my anxiety attack started, which was about 9:00 p.m. She came in and grabbed me as if she knew something. I was so hysterical at this point. My mother told me that she slapped me. I don't remember that to this day. Of course, I was drunk, but, I remember her telling me that whatever the problem was, I needed to tell her. By that time, I had calmed down a little. I told her that my father was cheating on her. I told her that my sister caught him over at the woman's house. It was devastating for me to have to tell my mom that, but she made me. However, believe it or not, it was also a huge burden lifted off me.

Suppression can be very dangerous. When you suppress your emotions, you become a walking volcano waiting to erupt. This is the danger of suppressing years of hurt and anger. As human beings, we are not equipped to bear burdens and uncontrolled emotions alone. God wants us to throw all our burdens and problems to Him because He is equipped to handle them. Peter tells us,

> ***"Humble yourself under the mighty hand of God, that He may exalt you in due time: Casting all your cares upon Him; for He careth for you" (1 Peter 5:6–7, KJV).***

He cares about us. Although we may experience things that we may not understand and things that hurt us badly, we have a God that is well able and waiting to see us through it all. It does not matter how old we are. Oftentimes, the pain is so bad that we turn to temporary fixes like alcohol, drugs, unhealthy relationships, illicit sex, etc. However, Jehovah Rapha, "God that heals" can heal you in every component of your life, which are spiritually, mentally, emotionally, physically. Understand that just as there is an appointed time to go through life's tragedies and misfortunes; there is an appointed time to come out! We must trust God enough to bring us through these times and, when He does, praise Him for it!

Some actions we take as parents can cause our children to become overwhelmed with unnecessary burdens. I say "unnecessary burdens" because these are burdens that children should not have to deal with. They do not have the power or ability to fix or change the situation, which oftentimes leads to depression and, sometimes, suicide. I encourage every parent to consider your entire family before making decisions that can affect them in a major way. Be careful of what you expose your children to or allow them to experience.

My mom later told me that when she came in and saw me that way, she knew that her life was getting ready to change forever. She said that even though I was the baby child, I was always the strongest;

and when she saw me like that, it had to be something great. She said that she would not have received that information from anyone else other than me.

Later, my parents ended up separating, and they eventually divorced. I became a very angry young lady. My brother and sister went their own way. I stayed with my mom and watched her go through all the hurt and pain. I suffered right along with her. I had no choice. I didn't have the power or ability to change a thing. I felt all her pain and misery. I hated my father for what he did to our family. He didn't just destroy our immediate family—he destroyed our entire extended family because our family was the center. We held most of the major family gatherings. We were once a close-knit family. Divorce is a death. It is the death of a family. After my mom and dad divorced, the family died. We all went our separate ways. The Browns were never as close as they used to be.

An affair is never just about the two people involved. It affects everyone who is tied to those two individuals. I felt as though the world and everything in it let me down. I felt abandoned and rejected. When a child feels abandoned or rejected, they believe that they have been forsaken, given up on, and deserted. It brings about a sense of insecurity. This is a dangerous place to be in. I adopted a self-destructive behavior. This is what tends to happen to individuals that do not know how to handle their emotions and are bitter in soul. I became a promiscuous teenager. I had a horrible attitude. I was full of hatred. My parents had been married for twenty-two years, and it was all gone to pieces. He walked away from our family to be with another family. He had gotten the other woman pregnant.

My world came crumbling down before me, and I didn't know what to do. I couldn't understand why all these things were happening to me. I started drinking hard alcohol and smoking marijuana. I started stealing from department stores and hanging with individuals that robbed people. I was carrying guns and had thoughts of suicide. I developed an "I don't care" mentality. The world owed me something, I thought. I'd become a very depressed young lady, but I managed to hide it well outside of the house. When I was at home, all I wanted to do was sleep because as long as I was sleeping, I didn't have to think about my problems. This is the number one sign of depression. My mother couldn't help me because she was messed up herself.

Life can be full of disappointments. We can be left to feel like we have been defeated in all of our expectations and hope. However, I had to understand—and so do you—that there was a greater picture beyond what I could see. Despite our heartaches and disappointments, God has a divine plan for our life. This is why somehow, we manage to pull through. If the truth be told, these things are written.

God tells us in His Word that His people are destroyed from a lack of knowledge.

> ***"My people are destroyed for lack of knowledge; because thou hast rejected knowledge, I will also reject thee, that thou shalt be no priest to me; seeing thou hast forgotten the law of God, I will also forget thy children" (Hosea 4:6, KJV).***

We destroy ourselves and others because we don't know God or the ways of God. We don't know God or His ways because we fail to seek Him daily, and in some cases, we don't believe in Him. So many people can't even abide by the simple golden rule, "Do unto others as you would have others do unto you," and yet they wonder why they and their children are cursed. The Bible declares that the way of a transgressor (one who sins against God) is hard.

> ***"Good understanding giveth favor: but the way of transgressors is hard" (Proverbs 13:15, KJV).***

When your back is against the wall, you don't know which way to turn, or you are being tempted with thoughts and emotions that you know are not of God, seek Him.

> ***Trust in the Lord with all thine heart, and lean not to thy own understanding. In all thy ways acknowledge Him, and He shall direct thy paths (Proverbs 3:5–6).***

We have to seek the knowledge of God. If we don't, we will become entangled with our own lusts and ungodly desires, thus destroying ourselves and our loved ones.

> ***And even as they did not like to retain God in their knowledge, God gave them over to a reprobate mind, to do those things which are not convenient; Being filled with all unrighteousness, fornication, wickedness, covetousness, maliciousness; full of envy, murder, debate, deceit, malignity, whisperers; Backbiters, haters of God, despiteful, proud, boasters, inventors of evil things, disobedient to parents,***

> ***Without understanding, covenant breakers, without natural affection, implacable, unmerciful: Who knowing the judgment of God, that they which commit such things are worthy of death, not only do the same, but have pleasure in them that do them. (Romans 1:28–31)***

Understand that life is never just about you and you alone. There are always consequences to our actions, whether our actions are good or bad. None of us is perfect. We will make mistakes. Let us acknowledge our faults and sins, repent, and seek God's direction for our lives. Let us allow God to heal our broken hearts and mend them back together.

To the husband or wife that may be contemplating an affair, please consider the many consequences. Pray and ask God to remove the feelings of lust and ungodly desires from your heart. He will do it. Ask Him to restore the passion and love that you once had for your spouse. He will do it. Then work on it. Yes, it takes work and effort. Date again. Have rendezvous. Invest in your marriage. It's yours—own it and take responsibility for it. You can't run from yourself. If you are having problems in your marriage and choose to divorce and eventually remarry, you better believe that you are going to have problems in the next marriage as well. They may be the same, they may even be different, but they will occur. The issue isn't problems.

Problems will always occur. The issue is learning how to deal with the problems and overcoming them. Marriage is a sacred commitment between a man and a wife that was instituted by God. The reason why there are so many failed marriages is because so many individuals try to succeed without making God the head of their marriage. He is the missing, but most important, piece in the success of many marriages. Unfortunately, many Christians do not have God as head of their marriages. Again, this is why there are so many failed marriages in the body of Christ. They confess Christ but deny the power thereof. They believe God to move in finances, healing, and other areas of deliverance. However, somewhere along the line, and for many reasons, many refuse to trust and believe God to save and heal themselves and their marriages.

I believe that humility is the key to any great deliverance. If we can humble and submit ourselves under the power and authority of God, then God can work out any deliverance that needs to take place in our lives. When you walk in humility, there is no room for pride. The Bible tells us that pride comes before destruction and a haughty spirit before a fall (see *Proverbs 16:18*). There are so many fallen marriages because of pride and/or not having God as the head.

When your marriage is a success, you and your family are a success. You don't have to be another statistic. God is able to deliver and heal your marriage, no matter where you are in the process. If you take heed to these words and are willing to make changes, He can move for you. I am not oblivious to the fact that there is an exception to every rule. There are many individuals that have lived right, holy, humble, and by the Word of God, and yet their spouse chose to step out of the boundaries of their marriage through unfaithfulness and chose to move on. In these cases, after you've done all you know to do, stand, and the God of our salvation will deliver you one way or another. We serve a great big God that can deliver us from any situation or circumstance that we may find ourselves in. Once you allow infidelity in, you have given way to the enemy and have broken your covenant between you, God, and your spouse. Remember, you have to deal with the consequences, which oftentimes are long term and affect so many people.

CHAPTER 3

The Deep Root of Rejection

Sometimes we go through such hard trials in our lives that the only thing we can think of is a way out or a way of escape, not knowing that what we are trying to escape is deeply embedded within us. At the age sixteen, a young man came into my life. At that time, I thought he was the answer to all my misery. He was everything that a young lady would want in a young man. He had the looks and sensitivity. He was there for me. He said all the right things. He provided for me. He filled the void that was in my life. The emotions that were involved were unexplainable. There was a love that we shared that was deeper than we could handle. He was my knight in shining armor. He was an unusual young man. He never cursed around me, he opened up the car door for me, he bought me gifts, always complimented me, etc. I truly loved him, and he truly loved me. We could talk about anything. We shared our past hurts with each other. The emotions we had and shared with each other were unexplainable. They were deep—as a matter of fact, too deep for teenagers. We really were not equipped to handle them. We poured every ounce of our emotions into each other, which created an ungodly soul tie because we poured our soul into each other. We didn't know it, but we became as gods to each other. We looked to each other to fill our needs, wants, voids, etc.

What we didn't know at the time was that the both of us had the root of rejection planted in us at some point in our past lives. Both of our fathers abandoned us, I as a teenager and he as a little boy. His father told him to go and pack a bag so he can go with him to Ohio, after begging him if he could go with him. He left him sitting on the porch all day waiting for him to come back from the store, only to be told that he wasn't coming back. There are many things that can cause the seed of rejection to take root. However, the love between us was real but unhealthy because God was not the center.

About a year and a half later, things took a dramatic turn. I started to come out of my shell and began to open up to others. I started to get back to the old me again. I felt anger and bitterness leaving me. I felt happy again. I began to notice that when I would be around others, laughing and enjoying myself, this young man would become upset. He wanted to be the only one to make me smile and laugh. He wanted to be my hero. The crazy part about this is he really was my world and my hero.

The root of rejection was in operation here. The fear of being rejected by me would set him off. Oftentimes, when we are afraid of being rejected as individuals, it is because of how we view ourselves. We view ourselves as being grasshoppers in the sight of others. We feel as though we need to perform all the time to please others; we tend to create our own fantasy world because it's easier to deal with. This is what rooted rejection can do to individual to say the least. It shows up at any time.

When one is abandoned, he or she often ends up with issues such as fear of rejection, inability to trust, suspicion, codependency, loneliness, shame, etc.

What many do not know is that when a person feels abandoned or rejected, especially as a child or teen, it takes a deep root. It begins as a simple seed that is planted by a negative experience in your life. It is the pain that comes with these negative experiences that often takes root and effect your way of thinking, living, and being. The root of rejection can distort the very person that you are. It was never God's intention for us to feel rejected. He loves us and desires for us to be and feel loved. The enemy has used the root of rejection to hinder, abort, and even stop God's people from coming into their very purpose in life. This is one of his greatest tactics. His goal is to cause many to remain bound by the root of rejection by suffering from low self-esteem, unresolved emotional wounds, feeling of inferiority, and undermining one's self worth. Without healing and deliverance, these things can lead to a miserable life of unforgiveness, anger, bitterness, jealously, fear of rejection, suspicion, insecurity, withdrawal, religion, legalism, condemnation, guilt, etc. None of these things exemplify the love of Christ that He desires for us. When you see someone dealing with either of these issues, you can almost always tie it to the root of rejection.

> ***"And to know the love of Christ, which passeth knowledge, that ye might be filled with all the fullness of God" (Ephesians 3:19).***

Let me share with you where the root of rejection can take you. The first time I tried to leave him, the abuse started. He told me that I could never leave him and that I was his forever. I later discovered that he was drug dealer. He managed to hide it from me during the course of our relationship. I didn't know what to think at this point.

One New Year's Eve night, I went over to his grandmother's house to meet with family and friends. We got into an altercation that would lead to his brother telling me that he'd never seen him act this way with any other girl. He told me that it would be difficult for me to leave him. I didn't know how to take that. I noticed that the only time that he would act this way was when I would leave or threaten to leave him. Other than that, he was the perfect young man. I didn't understand what that was all about at that time.

This brings us back to that root of rejection. This destroys the lives of so many. I often have said over the years that people, especially some parents, do not know what they do to an individual when they hurt others and deeply wound them by their actions or words toward them. Unless true and divine deliverance takes place, it can lead to life of turmoil.

There are a few daunting experiences that I recall that, like us, many individuals have gone through due to the issues within that stem from being rejected in life by those that had influence on us. Let me share.

One time, he took me downtown to a festival. It was late at night. He disappeared. We were walking, and he just disappeared. I had no idea where he went or what happened to him. I was so upset. I was downtown by myself. While I was walking, a few guys tried to come up to me, and I told them not to approach me. I was so angry and scared that I put my hand in my purse, grabbed our gun, and held a finger on the trigger the whole time.

Finally, he came from out of nowhere. He said that I was in his sight the whole time and that he just wanted to see if other guys would approach me if I was by myself. I was livid. His way of thinking was sometimes unbearable.

Rejection can distort your thinking. I told him to take me home and that it was over. We went back to the car. He started driving crazy. I told him that I hated that I was in this relationship. We got into it. He took me to an unfamiliar neighborhood—into a dark alley. He got out of the car and took me out. He locked the door, got back in the car, pulled off, and left in me a dark alley as he pulled down to the end and stopped. I was terrified. He backed back up, put me in the car, and told me that was how he felt when I tried to leave him. I just cried. The feeling made me feel miserable inside. The sad part was it was true. I loved him so much and understood the feeling of being rejected because I felt that way in so many ways as well, but I hated feeling that way and not knowing what I could do about it. In so many words, he wanted to make me feel the rejection that he was feeling, believing I would then understand. Hurting people hurt people even if they don't know the root cause of it; it's still a reality. In spite of the sad situation of two young people who truly were crazy about each other, but because of deeply rooted issues hurt each other, I felt trapped inside of myself and in this relationship. He too felt trapped. He was angry at himself for falling in love with me. He felt like it was easier not to love than to love and get hurt. Although I loved him, I knew that this was unhealthy, but I did not know how to leave. I loved him too much and was afraid to hurt him.

One time I decided to leave him. I wouldn't answer any of his calls. The truth being told, before I feared him, I would tell him that I was leaving him on purpose. I had a nasty attitude at times, and I knew what I was doing would provoke him. I could be manipulating at times, as many individuals with these issues are. However, things changed for me after I saw that he didn't take me leaving him lightly. There were so many more instances. I became so tired and knew this relationship wasn't healthy, but I was scared that if I tried to leave him that it would end in tragedy. The seed was growing. There was a time after I caught myself breaking up with him where he came to my house around three o'clock in the morning. I wouldn't open the door because I didn't know what he would do. He busted the door window and left. He called me over and over, asking me to come get him. I was afraid. I could hear his mother telling him to go to the ER before he bleeds to death. He told his mother that he wasn't going anywhere until I came and took him. As crazy as it may sound, I cared deeply for him; and believe or not, I took him. I was so drawn to him. We had a soul tie; although it was ungodly, it was still a soul tie. Our souls were tied together by our mind, emotions, and will.

When I got to his house, he was sitting on the couch with his hand over a bucket. Blood was everywhere. I took him to the ER, and he told them that I had done that to him. He finally told them the truth. I went and sat in my car. I cried, asking myself, *Why am I here?* I didn't understand the emotional soul tie, and I felt as though I had no control over who I was anymore. *Wow! Here is someone that I am crazy about, and now I'm confused because I know this is unhealthy for the both of us, and scared of being with him.* I felt trapped within. I felt like I had no power over my own body and mind. I stayed in the relationship because I loved him and had no power to leave. It was only at the threat of me leaving him that he would lose control. He would always say things like I was the only one who understood him, he could be himself around me, and that it was my fault that I made him fall in love with me. He could be himself around me. I saw a side that no one knew of. He was genuinely sweet, which was a side that most never seen of him. I thought I understood him, but I was just as messed up as he was. I actually loved being loved by him. I know it seems twisted, but it was our reality; and like many individuals, we needed Jesus and didn't know it.

There was a time when he came to my house and the telephone rang. He answered it, and it was one of my old male friends. He wanted me to tell him not to call me anymore. I wouldn't do it. He was upset and said that he was leaving. I was actually surprised that he didn't go into one of his rages. I believed that it would be that simple. I had become so numb that I don't think I even cared what he did anymore. I lay down and asked him to make sure to lock the door behind him. I dozed off to sleep.

Shortly after, I felt the presence of something over me and opened my eyes. We ended up having an altercation that could have ended up in a tragedy, but through the grace of God, He kept us from destroying ourselves and each other.

The last fight did it for me. I don't remember the cause of it; however, there is never a reason for a man and woman to have a physical confrontation—I always felt this way, yet I got caught in this web. This time it was different. We were fighting, and I actually had a vision of myself running in the kitchen, getting a knife, and seeing blood everywhere. Something was telling me to go grab a knife. I was terrified. I had become so terrified. I knew in my heart that love or not, we couldn't continue on like this. Have you found yourself or someone you may know in one of these stories yet? I share this for the purpose of you or someone you may know who is in need of deliverance. These issues are often overlooked and not talked about in the church. Generally, when we hear about them, it's too late.

Our lives had spiraled out of control. Our lives no longer belong to us anymore. Something greater had taken over. We had given each other too much power over our lives. This was a dangerous thing to do. We don't have life to give to someone else. Our life belongs to God and only God. He is our Creator.

> ***"Thus saith the LORD; Cursed be the man that trusteth in man, and maketh flesh his arm, and whose heart departeth from the LORD" (Jeremiah 17:5).***

We curse ourselves when we allow people to become our gods. This is what we are doing when we give man total control of our life. We had yielded ourselves to the enemy. The devil comes to kill, steal, and destroy God's people. One of his greatest tactics is to plant a seed of rejection before we can be developed in our mother's womb. He'd rather kill us, but he will settle for destroying us by destroying our mind, our way of thinking; instilling fear, insecurity; causing us to be anger, bitter, and filled with resentment, etc. When we are operating in either of these, we can never fulfill our divine purpose.

Somehow, that night ended. Shortly after that, when I was about nineteen or twenty, I was at home alone, crying. I was tired and didn't feel good about myself as a young lady. I was beautiful inside and out, but I didn't feel it at all. I felt ugly and worthless. It is impossible to feel good about yourself when you are dealing with the root of rejection. *How did I end up in this type of situation? Why did my father leave me? What did I do to cause all this?* I did not have the power to change, but I wanted my life back. It was an unhealthy relationship. I was angry and bitter with my dad. I was in sin. I needed Jesus. There were no mentors to be found. We needed help. I can recall how this young man would have us get down on our knees and pray quite often. This was so unusual to me. After every bad encounter we had, he would want to come together, if you know what I mean. It became a ritual. This was a relationship of two young individuals who loved each other but was bound by the root of rejection that was leading them to destruction.

I was lost within myself. I knew of God, but I didn't know God. I found myself in my bathtub one evening. I had never really prayed a prayer before—other than a good-night prayer—but this time, I prayed a sincere prayer. My heart was so heavy. I cried out to God and said, "Lord, please help me." I told God that if He didn't, I would probably end up dead or in jail, and I didn't want either. I truly felt in my heart that despite how we felt about each other, we needed to be apart. I felt that it would end in tragedy if God didn't intervene. We needed help. We had no power, and it was plain to see that the devil was set out to destroy us. We knew nothing about the warfare over our soul or of an adversary that was set out to destroy us before we could find out who we are in Christ. We knew nothing about being saved or having a spiritual covering. This was no unusual situation. Most people that have no idea that God has placed a high call on their lives have or will experience some turmoil and tragedy in their lives. The enemy is set out from the beginning of our lives to keep us from ever finding out that we are Kingdom citizens of God and have power and dominion over the things in the earth that would prevent us from walking in our divine purpose.

> ***"Be Sober, be vigilant; because your adversary the devil, as a roaring lion, walketh about, seeking whom he may devour" (1 Peter 5:8).***

I cried and cried until I fell asleep, and when I woke up, there was such a calmness and a peace that had come upon me that I couldn't understand at that time. Sometime later, he called and asked me to meet him at his aunt's house. Needless to say, I did. We spent the night together, and this would be the last night before our lives changed forever.

The next day, my phone rang. It was him. He said that he was in jail. He went to prison for many years. Only God can answer why things had to be this way, for I take no glory in another man's suffering, but I thank God that we are both alive and well today. God heard my prayer. I chose life not just for myself but for him as well. We both survived. Although my heart was broken, I always loved him. It was as if he had taken a large portion of my heart to prison with him. There was a sensitive side to him that only I saw even though I experienced that other side that was not healthy for us. Sometimes, prison can serve as an alternative to death, giving an individual a second chance at life. This can be a temporary safe haven for an individual to keep them from being killed in the streets and/or preserve them for purpose. In this case, God preserved him for purpose. I later heard that he gave his life to the Lord and served as an assistant pastor, elder, and mentor in prison. Many may say that this it was just jailhouse religion; however, I couldn't be a minister and not believe that God was able to deliver His people in the midst of their prison experience. God delivered Joseph out of prison and set him up in the palace.

> ***And Joseph's master took him, and put him into the prison, a place where the king's prisoners were bound: and he was there in the prison… And Pharaoh said unto his servants, Can we find such a one as this is, a man in whom the Spirit of God is? And Pharaoh said unto Joseph, Forasmuch as God hath shewed thee all this, there is none so discreet and wise as thou art. (Genesis 39:20, 41:38–39)***

God is a God of second chances. It is situations like this that pushes us into position for God to use us. It is what we do with our second chance that determines where we go in life. My prayer is that many individuals that are incarcerated will find God, have a life-changing experience, and that, upon their release, they find a great pastor to sit under, and allow God to use them to minister to men and women that are as they once were, just as God has used me to minister to many for the building of His kingdom. Unfortunately, most churches are not prepared to receive individuals that have been positioned for purpose.

I didn't have a relationship with God at that time, but He loved me enough to connect to me. I was broken and sincere.

"The Lord is nigh unto them that are of a broken heart; and saveth such as be of a contrite spirit" (Psalm: 34:18).

If you are sincere about your deliverance and being set free, God will hear you when you pray, no matter what state you find yourself in. These ungodly relationships are not healthy relationships of love. They are relationships built from rejection, brokenness, and unresolved issues of the heart. A man or woman can only love you the right way if they first love God the right way. This is nothing personal, but if a person does not love God or themselves, how can they love anyone? You need to love yourself as well. Don't get involved in an intimate relationship if you are not whole. This means to be complete and whole in all four components of life, which are spiritually, mentally, emotionally, and physically. If you are not, you will find yourself being pulled into your companion's world and losing yourself in the process.

A good example is my mom. She was my father's wife and our mother. She didn't have an identity of her own and lost herself in the process. If we would have stayed on the same path that we were on, we not only would have lost ourselves but possibly our lives. The both of you need help. If you love them, love them enough to pray and ask God to help you both. Both of your destinies are at stake! *You will find out later how God miraculously turned this situation around!*

As time went by, I found myself living out of the trunk of my car. I had previously tried to stay with family members, but it just didn't work out. Everything I owned was in the trunk of my car. I later ran into another young man whom I previously met in high school. He tried to date me then, but I totally wasn't interested. Here I was, living on broken pieces, getting into a relationship with someone. My heart was still broken and had been for years. It was never mended. I was torn apart from the love of my life. I hid my feelings and emotions. This was, sure enough, a setup for failure. I wasn't whole myself. I would go to his house to sleep while he worked at night. Beware of convenience situations!

One morning, I walked out of the house and realized that my trunk was open. Someone had broken into my trunk and had stolen everything I owned. They took all my belongings. I was devastated. I felt violated again. I had just started going to church and build up a wardrobe for church. There was a time before that you would have never caught me in a dress, but when I started going to church, I began to buy dresses. Now, everything I owned was gone. I was so discouraged. Oftentimes, when God is pulling on your heart to come to Him, the enemy sends people and situations your way to discourage, distract, or detour you from your purpose.

We had a lot of ups and downs. There was some abuse involved—both emotional and physical. He had a quick temper. He would snap at the twinkle of an eye and had a habit of grabbing me when he got angry. We had several of these types of confrontations. I saw myself repeating the same cycle. I couldn't help but think, *Things are not supposed to be this way for me. Why am I in this? How did I get here again?* I realized that I had been distracted from God. He delivered me out of the first situation, and I ended up in a similar situation. I was repeating the cycle. It was just like the children of Israel when God told them that they had been around Mount Seir way too long.

"Ye have compassed this mountain long enough; turn you northward" (Deuteronomy 2:3).

A deliverance that took them thirty-eight years should have only taken them eleven days. We can prolong our own deliverance by trying to do things our way. Finally, I couldn't take any more. I had taken all that I could. I left him. I was twenty-two years old. I started going back to church. This was where my heart was. You have to make decisions that are best for you. You count! You are somebody.

You do not have to suffer from all the negative issues that come along with rejection, for whom the Lord has set free is free indeed.

"If the Son therefore shall make you free, ye shall be free indeed" (John 8:36).

It will not be easy, but it will be worth your life, health, and strength. God started dealing with me a lot about getting my life right. I started losing my desire to hang out in the clubs. Yes, I did the clubs, hung out and got high—anything to try to fill the void. However, I became more laid-back and began to see things differently.

I realized that there is a space that God reserves just for himself. This space remains void until we allow God to fill it. Oftentimes, we spend years trying to fill this void with any and everything, only to realize later that unless we allow God to do it, we will never truly be whole.

After you are free from a relationship, there is a cleansing process that needs to take place. When you are emotionally and sexually involved with someone who is not your husband or wife, there is an ungodly soul tie to this person. In other words, your soul has become tied to this individual in one way or another, but it is not of God, and it is not approved by God.

If you have had multiple partners, then everyone that you have been sexually involved with becomes a part of you. This is why we have so many emotionally, mentality, and spiritually unstable individuals. It's ungodly and sinful. Sex is created for marriage. It is designed to bind a husband and wife closer to one another. There are emotions and passions that God has created for marriage only. This is why things get way out of control when two people who are not married are having sex. They can't handle the emotions that are involved because there is not a spiritual connection to bind them close together as God has intended. Therefore you must seek deliverance to become free and cleansed.

I got saved and didn't realize until then that I still had an ungodly soul tie with whom I had been with. I became purified through repentance—by the washing of water baptism into Jesus's name, by the renewing of my mind, and by seeking God by attending church regularly. I also prayed, fasted, and read the word of God consistently. You have to walk away from this sinful life, and this is the only way to remain truly free. Our old man is buried with Christ. In other words, when we are baptized in Jesus's name, we are symbolizing His death on the cross. The baptism pool serves as a liquid grave. As we go down into the water, we are burying our old man with Christ. As we come back up out of the water, we are walking into a newness of life. We are like newborn babes in Christ. We must now learn how to become more like Him.

> ***What shall we say then? Shall we continue in sin, that grace may abound? God forbid. How shall we, that are dead to sin, live any longer therein? Know ye not, that so many of us as were baptized into Jesus Christ was raised up from the dead by the glory of the Father, even so we also should walk in newness of life. Therefore we are buried with him by baptism into death; that like as Christ was raised up from the dead by the glory of the Father, even so we also should walk in newness of life. For if we have been planted together in the likeness of his death, we shall be also in the likeness of his resurrection: Knowing this, that our old man is crucified with him, that the body of sin might be destroyed, that henceforth we should not serve sin…For that wages of sin is death; but the gift of God is eternal life through Jesus Christ our Lord. (Romans 6:1–6, 23)***

We should dare not to go back into the life that God has delivered us from. Nothing is worth more than spiritual and emotional freedom. I encourage you to choose *life*.

CHAPTER 4

The Plot Unveiled

I attended a local church in Detroit, Michigan. Let me share my experience with you. On September 10, 1995, I was sitting in church and the bishop had just preached the morning message. He began the altar call. As he began to pull on the people's hearts, God was pulling on mine. I remember hearing something saying, "Today is your day." However, while this may sound amusing, I began to wrestle within myself. I had just gotten my hair done that Saturday, and I didn't want to mess up my hair getting baptized. I wrestled and wrestled and told myself, "Next week." There was a deacon in the baptism pool who later became my godfather.

As the bishop began to close out the altar call, the deacon said, "Excuse me, Bishop, but God is dealing with someone in here this morning." And when he said that, I jumped up and ran down to the altar, knowing that it was me. I felt as though the rest of my life depended on me giving myself to God that morning. I was baptized in Jesus's name that day. I went down in the water, and when I came up out of the water, I was praising God as though I had lost my mind. I had never praised God a day in my life, but something got a hold of me. I felt free. I felt resurrected. I felt clean. I felt pure. I felt whole.

I did not know that from that day forward, my life would change forever. I had made my first major transition, and that was converting from a sinner to Christianity. I stepped into the beginning of my destiny. God did a quick work in me. I began to realize that the devil's plot was to kill me, and if he couldn't do that, he would settle for taking my mind. However, God wanted to give me life. The plot was being unveiled.

> ***"The thief cometh not, but for to steal, kill, and destroy; I am come that they might have life, and that they might have it more abundantly" (John 10:10).***

God desires for us to live life and live it abundantly. There is a purpose for us all, and the enemy's job is to do anything he possibly can to keep us from fulfilling God's purpose and plan for our life. He knows that God has great plans for us. As a matter of fact, he tries to destroy us even before we can begin to tap into who we are.

> ***"Everyone that is called by my name: for I have created him for my glory, I have formed him; yea, I have made him" (Isaiah 43:7).***

One of the first things that I did as a newborn babe in Christ was call my father. I told you before that I hated him, so this was huge. I had been so angry with him. I hated to see him coming. I made sure that everyone knew that I hated him. I wanted him to hurt like I was hurting. However, after I gave my life to Christ, he was the first person I called. I felt so much love in my heart. This is what being born again does for us. It washes away our sins. When we accept Christ in our lives, we take on His attributes, and one of those attributes is love. We are able to see things as Christ does.

> ***"Jesus answered and said unto him, Verily, verily I say unto thee, Except a man be born again, he cannot see the kingdom of God" (John 3:3).***

It isn't until after we are born again that we are able to "see" the kingdom of God as Christ does.

Some attributes come immediately, and some come later. Some things fall off automatically, and others we have to work at. I let go all of the bitterness, hurt, and pain. I apologized to him for being angry with him all those years. I realized that I didn't have a heaven or hell to put anyone in; neither did I have the right not to forgive someone who had hurt me. Jesus went to the cross for the remission of our sins. He paid the price, so who are we not to forgive someone for their sins when the price has already been paid? My dad was so happy, and so was I. I felt liberated. When I let him out of bondage, I let myself out as well.

> ***"Therefore let it be known to you, brethren, that through this Man is preached to you the forgiveness of sins; and by Him everyone who believes is justified by the law of Moses, beware therefore, lest what has been spoken in the prophets come upon you" (Acts 13:38–40).***

Unforgiveness is like a cancer. It can eat at your soul. It is a form of bondage. You can never be complete or truly happy until you forgive those that have hurt you. I forgave my abusers. I prayed for them. They no longer have power over me.

The week I got saved, we happened to be in a revival. This is what I love about God—when He sets you up for a great deliverance, He knows how to do it well. God blessed my soul in this revival. Something got a hold of me during this great revival, and I knew that I would never be the same.

On that Friday night, a great woman of God by the name of Dr. Joyce Haddon was ministering. She called me out and told me about the great call of God that was on my life. I remember falling down, and she told the altar workers to stand me up because I needed to hear what she was about to tell me. She said that there was a unique and awesome anointing on me. If I may be honest, at that time, I did not know what she meant; however, God later revealed it to me. Now I understand why I went through so much as a young lady. The devil was trying to keep me from coming into the knowledge of who I really was in Christ. God had a plan. God has a plan for our lives even before we are formed in our mother's womb. It is called His determinant counsel...that which He predestined before the foundations of the world; no matter where we may find ourselves in life at God's appointed time for us to step into purpose, He will cause His angels to maneuver and manipulate situations and circumstances in our lives so that it will line up with His determinant counsel.

> ***"Before I formed thee in the belly I knew thee; and before thou camest forth out of the womb I sanctified thee, and I ordained thee a prophet unto the nations" (Jeremiah 1:5).***

Now, I am in no way insinuating that we are all called to be prophets to the nations; however, this serves as witness that before we are formed in our mother's womb, God has a divine purpose for our lives. I learned that it was a setup from the enemy since the beginning of my life, to try to keep me from ever getting to the place in which I had finally made it—the ark and safety of God's will and His divine plan. The enemy will try to take you out if he can. He does not want our eyes open to the great Kingdom plan that God has for us.

I remember going home that evening stirred up in the spirit. My telephone rang, and it was the young man I had left before I received Christ in my life. Somehow, I was not surprised. I told him that this call was of the devil. He told me that it wasn't. I asked him if he was saved, and he told me *yes*. I asked him if he had been baptized in Jesus's name, and he told me *no*. I told him that this call was of the devil and began to tell him all the great things that were happening to me in my spirit. I talked so much about what God was doing that he could not get a word in. Sometimes, you can't afford to let the enemy get a word in. He might trick you into going back, especially when you are not strong enough. You have to learn to cover and protect what God invests in your spirit.

He was on his break at work and asked me if he could call me back on his next break. I told him, "Yeah," but all I would talk about with him was God, and he agreed. He called me on his next break, and it was the same conversation—God and me. The next thing I remember was him calling me on his way home from work at about three o'clock in the morning. He told me that he wanted what I had. He said that he heard the peace in my voice and that was what he was looking for. He asked me if I would pray with him. Now, I had never prayed with anyone before. For that matter, I had never witnessed or ministered to anyone before. No one had ever personally witnessed to me or even shared a testimony with me. No one ever told me how God was working in their life and that I could have Him too.

Here it was. I have this man asking me to pray with him. I said, "Okay." I prayed with him. He was at a gas station on W14 Mile and Stephenson Highway just miles outside of Detroit. He got on his knees in the rain as we prayed. After we prayed, I told him that he would live by grace until that following Sunday and get baptized in Jesus's name, and that's what he did. I know it had to be God because I had no idea where the words came from. He started going to church. It wouldn't be a month that went by before he asked me to marry him. He told me that God said that I was his wife. I did not know the voice of God at that time. My thinking was "Who am I to say that God didn't say that?" So needless to say, we were married a few months later.

The purification process began—a process of being purged. To be purged is to be free from impurities. *To purge* is to purify, cleanse, remove impurities or other elements through cleansing, to rid of sin, guilt, or defilement, to cause an evacuation of the bowels. It is a spiritual cleansing. We have to purify ourselves from the things that once defiled us. This process is very important to a new Christian. The residue from the world is still on you, and in this process, you should begin to see a spiritual metamorphosis take place. There should be a change in your entire life. Our mind is just like a computer hard drive. Everything that we have taken in is stored on that hard drive. We now need a renewing of the mind by the washing of the Word of God. We have to cleanse our hard drive "mind" and begin to store what God had intended for us to store in for His will and purpose.

"Therefore if any man be in Christ, he is a new creature: old things are passed away; behold, all things are become new" (2 Corinthians 5:17).

"Let this mind be in you, which was also in Christ Jesus" (Philippians 2:5).

I told him that I would marry him on one condition. He had two sons—and they had different mothers. I told him that when we got one, we had to get the other, so that they would be raised up together. He agreed. After we got married, I gained two bonus sons, and we did just what we agreed. When we got one, we got the other. We got them on weekends, holidays, and summer vacation; and they grew up to love each other dearly and are, to this day, very close. I had to allow the Holy Spirit to minister to me on many occasions concerning my place in the boys' life. It is imperative that as a bonus parent, you remember that there is a purpose for God placing you in the lives of the children that He entrusts to you and placing in your life. God ministered to me the importance of being a stepparent. He showed me Joseph.

Now the birth of Jesus Christ was on this wise: When as his mother Mary was espoused

to Joseph, before they came together, she was found with child of the Holy Ghost.

Then Joseph her husband, being a just man, and not willing to make her a public example, was minded to put her away privily.

But while he thought on these things, behold, the angel of the Lord appeared unto him in a dream, saying, Joseph, thou son of David, fear not to take unto thee Mary thy wife: for that which is conceived in her is of the Holy Ghost.

And she shall bring forth a son, and thou shalt call his name Jesus: for he shall save his people from their sins.

Now all this was done, that it might be fulfilled which was spoken of the Lord by the prophet, saying,

Behold, a virgin shall be with child, and shall bring forth a son, and they shall call his name Emmanuel, which being interpreted is, God with us.

Then Joseph being raised from sleep did as the angel of the Lord had bidden him, and took unto him his wife:

And knew her not till she had brought forth her firstborn son: and he called his name Jesus. (Matthew 1:18–25)

God entrusted Jesus in the hands of Joseph to raise as his own son. This was a huge responsibility. Being a bonus parent is a huge responsibility, and God does not take it lightly. There is a purpose and plan even in raising children that did not come from your loins. It is our responsibility to seek God and find out what that purpose is. I was that example of what a true woman of God is to my bonus sons. It was not always peaches and cream. Many times, I felt left out, but I had to remember what my purpose was and love them as they were my own.

We must understand that no matter what we go through in this life, God has a divine purpose and a divine plan for our lives. No matter how bad the situation we are in at the moment may seem, there is a divine plan. In spite of all the things I endured and would endure, I am victorious, for I know now that what Satan meant for evil, God meant for my good.

> ***"But as for you, ye thought evil against me; but God meant it unto good, to bring to pass, as it is this day, to save much people alive" (Genesis 50:20).***
>
> ***"And we know all things work together for good to them that love God, to them who are the called according to his purpose" (Romans 8:28).***

God desires that no one perishes. He wants all of us to make it through despite our faults—even those who have hurt us.

> ***"The Lord is not slack concerning his promise, as some men count slackness; but is long suffering to us-ward, not willing that any should perish, but that all should come to repentance" (2 Peter 3:9).***

CHAPTER 5

Identity Transition

A *transition* is when you go from the place where you are to a place that you have never been to, or even seen, before. The identity transition is a vital stage for a Christian.

> ***"Therefore if any man be in Christ, he is a new creature: old things are passed away; behold, all things are become new" (2 Corinthians 5:17).***

New creature means new identity because as new Christians, we are no longer the individuals that we once were. When we are new in Christ, we have to find out who we are in Him. When you have never been saved before and don't know anything about being saved, this is like a culture shock. We are fresh out of the world and fresh into Christianity, and as for me, I don't mean by word only but also by deed. I was truly living the life that I confessed in Christ. I was thriving in the midst of uncertainty. This brought about a sense of insecurity within both of us. I wasn't the Karen that I used to be, and he wasn't the person that he used to be. So now, we each had to find out who we were. We not only had to get to know ourselves as a new individual, but we had to get to know each other as these new individuals as well. I can't tell you about all his personal transitions or experiences, but what I can tell you that there were several times in his walk in Christ where he had taken a backslidden state, which pushed me into position of prayer on many levels and many occasions. I most certainly can tell you about mine and some that we had together. I can tell you about the things we had to encounter during this phase of transition.

In the very beginning of our marriage, we both lost our jobs through no fault of our own. Our phone was disconnected for about four months. At first, we didn't know what was happening. However, now I understand that God was placing us into a position to seek Him and trust Him. It is important to remember that everything bad is not of the devil. God shields us in seasons so that we can become grounded and rooted in Him for transition that is needed to take place in our lives so that the enemy does not have easy access to us. He shields us from the outside world that would try to pull us back in and from the forces and influences that once had power over us. God is our shield and protector.

> ***"He shall cover thee with his feathers, and under his wings shalt thou trust: his truth shall be thy shield and buckler" (Psalm 91:4).***

My hunger and thirst after God's righteousness began to grow.

> ***"Blessed are they which do hunger and thirst after righteousness: for they shall be filled" (Matthew 5:6).***

I began to seek God in a way that I never sought him before. I attended Bible Academy. I attended every church service. I attended every preaching engagement that our bishop had. I became faithful to the ministry. I cleaned the church. I joined the choir. I led praise and worship. I wasn't the best, but I was available. I traveled over the highways with the church, in state and out of state. As I did this, I found myself wanting more of God. I would encourage every believer to find a good church home where you find yourself growing in the Lord and become faithful to that ministry. The more you seek after God, the more he reveals Himself to you, and the more you become like Him. There was something that had taken a hold of me. God ordered my steps.

Before God saves us, we are people who are lost but find our way to Christ by faith through his grace and mercy.

> ***"For by grace were ye saved through faith; and that not of yourselves: it is the gift of God" (Ephesians 2:8).***
>
> ***"The steps of a good man are ordered by the Lord: and he delighteth in his way" (Psalm 37:23).***

As time went by, I became grounded and rooted in the Lord. God began to show me who I was in Him. I became a praiser for God. I appreciated Him for snatching me out of the devil's mouth. He was surely eating me alive. Through much prayer and fasting, God began to build me up in the faith, and I began to realize that there was ministry in me and that there was something greater for me. My husband at that time was ordained as deacon after about two years of being faithful to the ministry. He served in many areas of ministry, spreading himself very thin. It wouldn't be long after that he began to slack in his prayer and consecration life while still fulfilling the needs of the ministry. Needless to say, this put a strain on our marriage. It is very important that as an individual in ministry, you make sure that your service to ministry does not supersede your prayer and consecration life. You will fall into the very trap that has been laid from the foundations of the earth by the enemy...the lust of the eye, the lust of the flesh, and the pride of life. It is only when we are living a prayerful and consecrated life that we can defeat the enemy of temptation.

> ***Then was Jesus led up of the Spirit into the wilderness to be tempted of the devilAnd when he had fasted forty days and forty nights, he was afterward an hungred.***
>
> ***And when the tempter came to him, he said, If thou be the Son of God, command that these stones be made bread.***
>
> ***But he answered and said, It is written, Man shall not live by bread alone, but by every word that proceedeth out of the mouth of God.***
>
> ***Then the devil taketh him up into the holy city, and setteth him on a pinnacle of the temple,***

> ***And saith unto him, If thou be the Son of God, cast thyself down: for it is written, He shall give his angels charge concerning thee: and in their hands they shall bear thee up, lest at any time thou dash thy foot against a stone.***
>
> ***Jesus said unto him, It is written again, Thou shalt not tempt the Lord thy God.***
>
> ***Again, the devil taketh him up into an exceeding high mountain, and sheweth him all the kingdoms of the world, and the glory of them;***
>
> ***And saith unto him, All these things will I give thee, if thou wilt fall down and worship me.***
>
> ***Then saith Jesus unto him, Get thee hence, Satan: for it is written, Thou shalt worship the Lord thy God, and him only shalt thou serve.***
>
> ***Then the devil leaveth him, and, behold, angels came and ministered unto him. (Matthew 4:1–11)***

I later became a deaconess, missionary, and later answered the call to evangelism. I understood at this point why I went through some of the horrible things that I had gone through. There was a great purpose for my life. Understand that the devil never stops trying to stop you from discovering your purpose and fulfilling your destiny. He just changes methods. The tests and the trials began to come, but I praise God for the wonderful counselor—mighty God and the Prince of peace that He is—and how He began to minister to my soul. I can't stress enough how important it is to establish a consistent prayer life. This is what gives you the strength and the ability to sustain.

> ***"Praying always with all prayer and supplication in the Spirit, and watching thereunto with all perseverance and supplication for all saints" (Ephesians 6:18).***
>
> ***"Confess your faults one to another, and pray one for another, that ye may be healed. The effectual fervent pray of a righteous man availeth much" (James 5:16).***

God has chosen to use many individuals like you and me. The problem comes with the spirit of inconsistency. While God desires to use many of the saints, he can't because there is such a lack of consistency. He can't use these types of individuals in the capacity that He desires to because He has too much to invest. He will not invest all that He has to invest in a seasonal saint. God needs to know that He can trust you once you realize who you are in Him. As you take on the identity of Christ, your life is hidden in Him. The old man is buried with Christ the moment you go down in Jesus's name through baptism.

> ***"For ye are dead, and your life is hid with Christ in God" (Colossians 3:3).***

CHAPTER 6

Embrace the Process

As time went by, I began to realize who I really was in Christ. I was a woman of God.

> ***But rise, and stand upon thy feet: for I have appeared unto thee for this purpose, to make thee a minister and a witness both of these things which thou hast seen, and of those things in the which I will appear unto thee: Delivering thee from the people, and from the Gentiles, unto whom now I send thee, To open their eyes, and to turn them from darkness to light, and from the power of Satan unto God, that they may receive forgiveness of sins, and inheritance***

> ***among them which are sanctified by faith that is in me. (Acts 26:16–18)***

Through the love of Christ, I began to learn how to love. He placed me under great spiritual leaders. They played a great role in teaching many how to love God, myself, others, and my family.

However, I understood that there was an adversary that does not want us to fulfill our purpose and destiny. There were several years of trials and tribulations as God began preparing me for a greater ministry.

> ***"Be sober, be vigilant; because your adversary the devil, as a roaring lion, walketh about, seeking whom h may devour" (1 Peter 5:8).***

One day, I was in prayer in my basement, which was my secret place, and God began to speak to me. He told me that He had me in the midst of transition, and that He was getting ready to take me from the place where I was to a place that I had never seen or been before. He told me that I was in the midst of the process.

A *process* is a series of actions, functions, or events that bring about a certain result or end. He said that He needed me to "embrace the process," and that if I did not embrace this process, the devil would come and try to knock me off my mark, try to discourage me, and try to steer me from my destiny.

To *embrace* is to grab hold of, to cleave to, to hold to your bosom with all your heart, soul, and might. I thank God for the covering of a pastor. In this season in my life, he came to me and told me that God was going to birth messages in me through my tests and trials, and that's exactly what happened. God told me to embrace this process because it was going to take me to my destiny. So I began to pray, fast, and study the Word of God.

In the beginning of our marriage, we would go to our pastor for much counseling, but after a while, it was time to grow up. It was time to get in touch with God and come into our own personal relationship with Him. It was time to trust God to show us how to grow. Our pastor began to wean us away from him slowly. This was probably the best thing that he could do for us. A good leader knows you have to step back at some point in your members' walk with Christ and allow them to grow up and establish a relationship with God.

There is only one God, and if you're not careful, leaders can become as a god to their members. No one should seek man more than they seek God; as members, we should understand that God has placed pastors in our lives to give us spiritual inheritance and guidance. They are to impart knowledge and wisdom and guide us by leading by example. Our leaders should be of integrity and character. They should be known in the gates as living a clean and holy life. Our leaders can only carry us so far. After a while, we have to learn to walk on our own two feet.

> ***For when the time ye ought to be teachers, ye have need that one teach you again which be the first principles of the oracles of God; and are become such as have need of milk, and not of strong meat. For every one that useth milk is unskillful in the word of righteousness: for he is a babe. But strong meat belongeth to them that are of full age, even those who by reason of use have their senses exercised to discern both good and evil. (Hebrews 5:12–14)***

The enemy tried to use my marriage to break me on many occasions. In many circumstances concerning these trials, the enemy thought he won, but it only pushed me to a higher place of prayer. He made me seek God. I had to grow up in the spirit. It is vital that as an individual in Christ, when the tests and trials come your way, you learn to go to God in prayer. This is a spiritual weapon of mass destruction. One day in prayer, God took me to Genesis.

> ***Now the Lord said unto Abram, Get thee out of thy country, and from thy kindred, and from thy father's house unto a land that I will show thee: And I will make of thee a great nation, and I will bless thee, and make thy name great; and thou shalt be a blessing: And I will bless them that bless thee, and curse him that curseth thee: and in thee shall all families be blessed. (Genesis 12:1–3)***

It's not always that we are to leave the ministry. God wants us learn to trust Him to guide us and lead us throughout of lives. God called Abram out from his father's house to establish a covenant with him. It was only through faith and trust in God that Abram would reach his destiny. Our lives and destiny are predicated on obedience. Like Abram we have to embrace the process. It is embracing the process that will take you to your destiny. We have to understand that finding out who we are in God, what our purpose is, and fulfilling our destiny is not just for us but for others as well. We must understand that when we are called to a great work in Christ, God has individuals waiting for us to show up in their lives to be set free. So we don't have the pleasure, or the time, to play church. We must be about our father's business.

> ***"And when they saw him, they were amazed: and his mother said unto him, Son, why hast thou thus dealt with us? Behold, thy father and I have sought thee sorrowing. And he said unto them, How is it that ye sought me? Wist ye not that I must be about my Father's business?" (Luke 2:48–49).***

Jesus knew His purpose and did not waste time in being about God's will. He understood the importance of doing the will of Yahweh. We have to learn to walk closely to God by building and establishing a prayer life and set up a spiritual altar in our homes. Abram built an altar (a place of prayer, a place of elevation, a place where man meets and talks with God) to God after he began his journey.

> ***"And the Lord appeared unto Abram, and said, Unto thy seed will I give this land: and***

there builded he an altar unto the Lord, who appeared unto him" (Genesis 12:7).

However, if we read further, we find that Abram began to travel, and there was a famine in the land, which represents trials and tribulations. This also can represent a dry place in your life. Abram decided to go to Egypt, which represented worldliness. However, in going to Egypt, he feared for his life in that they would want his wife and try to kill him because she was beautiful, so he convinced his wife to lie and say that she was his sister.

And there was a famine in the land: and Abram went down into Egypt to sojourn there; for the famine was grievous in the land. And if came to pass, when he was come near to enter into Egypt, that he said unto Sarai his wife, Behold now, I know that thou art a fair woman to look upon: Therefore it shall come to pass, when the Egyptians shall see thee, that they shall say, This is his wife: and they will kill me, but they will save thee alive. Say, I pray thee, thou art my sister: that it may be well with me for thy

> ***sake; and my soul shall live because of thee. (Genesis 12:10–13)***

So they compromised and lied. He said that Sarai was his sister so that the Egyptians would not kill him. Abram received all kinds of gifts, and they treated him well. The world will readily receive you if you deny Christ. However, God was angry and sent a plague (an affliction or calamity) on Pharaoh's house. Pharaoh knew what happened and sent Abram and his family out of Egypt. The world will readily reject you if you cause a problem for them as well. No situation is worth compromising. God will never leave you or forsake you.

> ***"Let your conversation be without covetousness; and be content with such things as ye have: for he hath said, I will never leave thee, nor forsake thee" (Hebrews 13:5).***

God was trying to teach us that we must learn to trust Him no matter what things may look like. He wanted us to see how important it is to stay close to the altar and close to Him. When we move away from the place of the altar, the place of prayer, it is then that we find ourselves vulnerable enough to compromise God's Word. Thank

God for His grace and mercy that would lead us back to that first place, which is the altar, even after we have gone astray.

> ***"And he went on his journeys from the south even to Beth-el, unto the place where his tent had been at the beginning, between Beth-el and Hai; Unto the place of the altar, which he had made there at the first: and there Abram called on the name of the Lord" (Genesis 13:3–4).***

Notice how it says he went back to the place where he had been in the beginning—the place which he had made there at first. This is very important because we should always find ourselves seeking God like we sought Him when we were babes in the Lord. We must grow up, however, having a mind to seek God with humbleness and the innocence of a child.

> ***And Jesus called a little child unto him, and set him in the midst of them, and said, Verily I say unto you, except ye be converted, and become as little children, ye shall not enter into the kingdom of heaven. Whosoever there-***

> ***fore shall humble himself as this little child, the same is greatest in the kingdom of heaven. (Matthew 18:2–4)***

This is where embracing the process becomes important. As the trials and tribulations came, the persecution came. Folk began to lie and make false accusations against me. I would hear rumors concerning me, but I learned to embrace the process. In this process, I learned that people will actually lie about you. I couldn't believe it. I saw church people do people worse than worldly people do each other. Then I learned that anyone is capable of being used by the enemy if we are not careful. Nevertheless, God always reveals the truth.

The devil became very bold…There was a minister that came to me one day and told me that he was in love with me and had been for years. I told him that the devil was a liar and that the plot was not just against him and me but against my husband, his wife, and our children. I ministered to him and sent him on his way. While it may seem flattering, we can't afford to entertain those types of thoughts and spirits. The devil is an opportunist and waits for the perfect opportunity to get in. Usually in marriage, he tries to come when the couple is at odds with each other. This is why it is so important that you communicate with each other, resolve your issues in a timely fashion, and get on one accord.

There was also a young woman that pursued my husband. She would call him all the time when she and her husband were having problems. I didn't mind because I thought that she was sincere at the time. He said he realized that she had other intentions when she invited him over and said that her husband would not be there. He rejected her offer. Shortly after that, I received a phone call from her with an accusation from her and her husband. The accusation was so out there that I laughed. However, I called my husband with the both of them on the phone, and of course, he denied it. While they were all going at it, I just listened then told them thanks for calling, but I was running late for Bible study. I didn't even go there. I maintained my integrity, character, and spirituality. I prayed about it, and the Lord revealed the truth. Her husband apologized to my husband about the lie and told him why they did it. It was a lesson to the both of us, as well, on how to use wisdom when ministering to the opposite sex. Maybe somehow, we led these individuals on. The Bible tells us to be wise as serpents and harmless as doves.

> ***"Behold, I send you forth as sheep in the midst of wolves: be ye therefore wise as serpents, and harmless as doves" (Matthew 10:16).***

The young lady that pursued my husband later came to me and told me that she had watched me over the years and that if there was anyone that she desired to be like, it was me. I tried stopping her; however, she said that she needed to tell me what she had to tell me. She went on to say that she knew that I was a true woman of God. What the enemy meant for evil, God turned it around for our good. I still maintained my character and integrity through the persecution, and in doing so, people were able to see Christ in me. I share these instances with you so you will know how serious these matters are. The devil is not playing with us. I encourage you who are reading this book to take your walk with Christ seriously because lives are at stake here.

There was a time in my life when I could not conceive children. The doctors told me that I would never have children. This was due to the trauma my body had suffered as a child. I was a modern-day Hannah. The enemy provoked me in this area, as he did Hannah. It can be very devastating wanting to have a baby, but not being able to because of no fault of your own. I had folk calling me, telling me that they were pregnant and asking me if we wanted the baby because they didn't want it. One evening, I went to the book of 1 Samuel in the Word of God.

"And she vowed a vow, and said, O Lord of hosts, if thou wilt indeed look on the affliction of thou handmaid, and remember me, and not forget thine handmaid, but wilt give unto thine handmaid a man child, then I will give him unto the Lord all the days of his life, and there will not razor come upon his head" (1 Samuel 1:11).

I told God that I believe every word that is in the Word of God. I embraced this process. I cried out to him just as Hannah did. I even prayed a similar prayer and made the same covenant that Hannah made. Yes, I told God that if He would bless me with a child, that I would give it back to Him. In the time the Old Testament was written, that meant that parents would give their baby to the High Priest to raise in the House of God. I meant that I would raise my child up in the church and in the way of holiness. Shortly after that, a woman of God by the name of Pastor Daffin spoke in my life. She told me, at one point in my life, I cursed myself. She said that I said that I did not want to have any children. She was absolutely right. I said that in my bitterness state, when I was angry with my father for abandoning us. We must understand that words have power, and the power of life and death is in the tongue.

"Death and life are in the power of the tongue: and they that love it shall eat the fruit thereof" (Proverbs 18:21).

She prayed for me. Some things we must go back and undo. She told me that I would conceive in three months, and in three months, I conceived. I remember the day of my first ultrasound. We had a terrible, heated argument. I walked all the way to my father's house to borrow their car. I drove myself there. I was five months pregnant at that time. I was in having the ultrasound done, and the ultrasound tech called the doctor in. They were collaborating with each other very quietly. The doctor asked me when had I heard my baby's heartbeat last. I told them I went to the doctor six days ago when I saw my doctor, and everything was good. They told me that my baby was dead. I couldn't believe it. This was so devastating to me. After finally arriving and hearing the news, my husband at that time had to almost literally carry me out of the place.

I went for a second opinion and received the same news. This time, they told me that I had to be induced for labor. I was admitted into the hospital, and when the nurse came to induce me, I told her to wait a minute. There was something I had to do. I went in the bathroom and cried; however, I praised God for honoring His part of the promise. In spite of my pain, I realized that there was a time when I could not conceive, and God honored His part. He allowed me to conceive. I just did not realize that in honoring my part of the covenant that I had to give my baby back to Him in that way. I thought I could raise her up in the church. Yes, I later found out that the baby was a girl. I was devastated by the loss, but I still learned to praise God in my affliction. The Bible says, in all things, give thanks.

> ***"In everything give thanks: for this is the will of God in Christ Jesus concerning you" (1 Thessalonians 5:18).***

I was so grateful to know that I was at least able to conceive. I was thankful for my church family during this process. They came and cooked and cleaned for me. They ministered to my needs. Five months later, I conceived again. This time, God gave me double for my trouble, and I successfully gave birth to two beautiful, healthy identical twin boys. Hallelujah!

The first message I preached came as a result of this experience, "Thank God for Peninnah. It was through this trial and tribulation that I learned that if you praise God through whatever you are going through, no matter how much it hurts you, you can come out victorious. It was through this trial that I learned to praise God for my enemies, my adversaries, my hurts, my pains, and my wounds. I learned that these things will push you to a place in prayer and to a place in God that you probably would not otherwise have obtained. This is where I really began to learn to embrace the process. I pushed into prayer beyond the veil. I learned to come out of the outer courts, which is the place where you are still dwelling in the fleshy realm. I had to press into the inner courts, which is that place where you are not quite out of the fleshly realm but you are somewhat entering to the spiritual realm. This is that place where spiritual warfare takes place. This is where the enemy hangs out. He can't go any farther than this realm. He can't enter into the Holy of holies or Most Holy as some call it. The Holy of holies is the divine presence of God. This is that place that we can enter into where we hear from God, where we get our answers from Elohim. I made it to this place in prayer by pressing beyond my hurt, pain, tribulation, and seeking the divine presence of our Heavenly Father.

The Lord gave me revelation on the spirit of "Peninah." He walked me back through my entire life, quickly pointing out a lot of things I had gone through since I was a little girl. He said that this spirit was designed to make me feel less than, inferior, unworthy; but in retrospect, it was afraid of what was in me and what I would birth forth. Understand that the spirit of "Peninnah" is a xenophobic spirit (*fear and hatred of strangers or foreigners or of anything that is strange or foreign*). In others words, because you are not an easy read, or can't be controlled and manipulated, it is afraid of who you are or what you may birth forth.

> ***"And her adversary also provoked her sore, for to make her fret, because the LORD had shut up her womb. And as he did so year by year, when she went up to the house of the LORD, so she provoked her; therefore she wept, and did not eat" (1 Samuel 1:6–7).***

The Bible says that Hannah's adversary "Peninnah" provoked her sore…In other words, she mocked her, irritated her, ridiculed her—you name it—and the real reason was because she was afraid of what was in her. However, Hannah got tired of being provoked yearly and had gotten to a place where she was pushed (forced) to press into a realm in the spirit where God would hear here petition. She got so caught up in the realm of the spirit that the priest thought she was drunk. Sometimes, we have to get so caught up in prayer that we lose ourselves in the spirit. This is where we get God's attention.

Hannah gave birth to the prophet Samuel. This is what that spirit was afraid of.

> ***So Hannah rose up after they had eaten in Shiloh, and after they had drunk. Now Eli the priest sat upon a seat by a post of the temple of the LORD. And she was in bitterness of soul, and prayed unto the LORD, and wept sore. And she vowed a vow, and said, O LORD of hosts, if thou wilt indeed look on the affliction of thine handmaid, and remember me, and not forget thine handmaid, but wilt give unto thine handmaid a man child, then I will give him unto the LORD all the days of his life, and there shall no razor come upon his head. And it came to pass, as she continued praying before the LORD, that Eli marked her mouth. Now Hannah, she spake in her heart; only her lips moved, but her voice was not heard: therefore Eli thought she had been drunken. And Eli said unto her, How long wilt thou be drunken? put away thy wine from thee. And Hannah answered and said, No, my lord, I***

> ***am a woman of a sorrowful spirit: I have drunk neither wine nor strong drink, but have poured out my soul before the Lord. Count not thine handmaid for a daughter of Belial: for out of the abundance of my complaint and grief have I spoken hitherto. Then Eli answered and said, Go in peace: and the God of Israel grant thee thy petition that thou hast asked of him. And she said, Let thine handmaid find grace in thy sight. So the woman went her way, and did eat, and her countenance was no more sad. And they rose up in the morning early, and worshipped before the Lord, and returned, and came to their house to Ramah: and Elkanah knew Hannah his wife; and the Lord remembered her. Wherefore it came to pass, when the time was come about after Hannah had conceived, that she bare a son, and called his name Samuel, saying, Because I have asked him of the Lord. (1 Samuel 1:9-17)***

Many people have had to deal with individuals treating them badly for this very reason. Many of you are pregnant with purpose, and for this very reason, you have been fought on every hand to keep you from coming into your greatness. However, what God has ordained for our lives, if we be in Christ, we shall fulfill that which He has promised.

Shortly after the twins were born, the hype was over. The enemy came in like a flood. After everything had calmed, I realized that the enemy had set up camp in my house while I was on maternity leave. My husband had begun to slip away from God. I had to go into spiritual warfare just to have a piece of mind. I remember putting the babies to sleep praying and crying out to God on many occasions. I felt him slipping away from God, even though he went to church every Sunday. He was an officer in church, but he covered well. No one knew what was going on. I saw it. I had to deal with it at home. I didn't have time for maternity leave. I had to go to warfare. I had to embrace this process. I remember fighting so in the spirit until I just got tired of fighting. I started praising God like I had lost my mind to keep from losing my mind.

Praise is another major weapon of mass destruction. Sometimes when you are all spent out on praying, you have to revert to praise mode in order to build yourself back up. My husband had become so carnal minded that I could not even stand him anymore. He was living one way at home and acting another way in church. I became bitter toward him, and he was bitter toward me. I refused to be married to a jackleg deacon. I did not know him anymore. He would take every opportunity that he could to belittle me, mock me, or talk about me negatively to others. I would walk up on him with some of the sisters in the church, and he'd be talking about me. I was tired of praying for him. I began to pray that he would go outside the marriage so that I could be free. For all I knew, he probably had already gone outside the marriage; we were so disconnected. Yes, I did. I believed that I married Ishmael and missed out on my Isaac. Isaac was the promise, and Ishmael was the compromise. I even told him that one time. I thought that a husband was supposed to cover, intercede, and take care of his wife. Here I was, stuck at home with two babies all day interceding for a man that I no longer wanted to be married to. Something was wrong with this picture.

One day, God sent a word that if I speak to the king in the man, I would bring out the king in the man, and if I speak to the fool in the man, then I would bring out the fool in the man. I know that was God because I was surely speaking to the fool in this man. I repented. I cried out before God. I knew my spirit was not right. Even though I felt justified at the time, I was wrong. We are accountable for our own actions. I managed to pull myself together. God told me in my secret place that if I worked on myself, He would take care of him. So, I began to cleanse myself. I had been guilty of walking in the flesh. We have to work out our own salvation with fear and trembling.

> ***"Wherefore, my beloved, as ye have always obeyed, not as in my presence only, but now much more in my absence, work out your own salvation with fear and trembling" (Philippians 2:12).***

At that point, I had come to a place where I had wanted a divorce. However, I knew that my spirit was not right. I had made up in my mind that I was going to get back in the presence of God and seek healing, deliverance, and an answer. I wanted to make sure that my spirit was pure and that I was right before God before making any major decisions. Never make major decisions when you are emotional because emotions change, depending on your circumstances. Many individuals have made major decisions and then had a change in emotions, only to realize that they can't reverse their actions. As individuals, we must understand that we do not have the ability to change people, but we have the ability to change ourselves. We must be careful not to allow what we are going through to kill our spirit man and turn us into something we do not want to become. It is not acceptable to God to treat people bad because they are treating us bad. It feels like the right thing to do. However, when we truly allow the Holy Spirit to abide in us, how can we treat others bad? If Christ truly abide in us and us in Him, it would be impossible.

I began to work on myself. This was all a part of transition and embracing the process. These are the things that would eventually take us into our destiny. We have to learn to humble ourselves, trust, and hearken to the voice of God if we plan to keep moving forward in Him.

> ***"And thou shalt remember all the way which the Lord thy God led thee these forty years in the wilderness, to humble thee, and to prove thee, to know what was in thine heart, whether thou wouldest keep his commandment or no" (Deuteronomy 8:2).***

We should never allow ourselves to get so angry or frustrated with someone that we allow them to pull us out of the will of God. I had found myself just as guilty as I thought he was by allowing my anger and bitterness toward him to sabotage my relationship with God. So, the least I could do was humble myself before God to prove to God that I loved Him more than what anyone thought of me. I had no idea what to expect of my marriage. We had been at odds with each other for a while. It had been like living with a stranger. However, I was to the point that if he looked at me and said that he didn't want to be married to me anymore, I would have been just fine. I had gotten myself to place where I just wanted my spirit and soul to be right with God. This is what God is looking for. This is the place where we need to be in order for God to reveal His glory in our life.

> ***"Ye are my witnesses, saith the LORD, and my servant whom I have chosen: that ye may know and believe me, and understand that I am he: before me there was no God formed, neither shall there be after me" (Isaiah 43:10).***

It is not about who's right or wrong or who will break first. It is about God getting the glory and being set free.

Shortly after, he found himself in a place of persecution. This place just brought him closer to the Lord at the time. This was a process that he had to embrace. This process broke him and humbled him. I told you that God always has a plan of deliverance.

Abraham ended up becoming the father of the nation. God used him in a mighty way. It is because of him we are children of the promises of God. He encountered a lot, but he embraced the process that would lead many to the covenant promises of God.

CHAPTER 7

Weep Not for Me

As time went by, I became pregnant with my third child. I could still see the enemy. Every time I turned around, it was one thing after another. One evening, I was in my basement, praying; and as I was praying, I began to think about everything that I had gone through. I cried out to the Lord...*Lord! What is it about me? What is it that the enemy knows about me that I didn't know about myself?*

Oh, but one night, I was on St. Simons Island in Brunswick, Georgia, in one of our national church conference. I received one of the greatest deliverances of my life, and that was from people. I had been so hurt and disappointed in finding out that people in church can be just as bad, if not worse, than people in the world. I was seven months pregnant with my baby.

God had given me instructions to get up, get myself together, and go to the restaurant in the hotel where we were staying. I had been in the room for hours alone. So, I did just what I was instructed. I got up after a nap. I got myself together for church service. I went to the restaurant, sat down at a table, and ordered my food. Shortly after that, the bishop came walking in. He was with his grandchildren. He sat them down at a table and came and sat at my table for a minute.

He looked at me and asked me what I was doing sitting at the table by myself. I just looked up at him. He began to speak to my spirit man. He said, "Woman of God, you have been so misunderstood, and it's because you don't say much. You hold things in and don't talk to anyone. You need to find someone you can trust to open up to." Tears just flowed down my face. He blessed my soul. He ministered to me. I can't stress enough how important it is to be obedient to the voice of the Lord. That was me. I couldn't trust everyone with the issues. They were personal, and I didn't want to put my business out like that. I had been hurt by people that I trusted, so it was difficult to trust anyone to share my deepest wounds with. There was so much I had been holding in. Some things I just couldn't talk about because of the people that were involved.

That evening, I went to the conference, and the spirit of the Lord came into the place and delivered me from the bondage of people. I had to learn that people can hold you in bondage if you let them. We have to get away from trying to understand how people can be the way that they are. We have to learn to forgive and move forward. I learned how not to take things personal. It was all a part of the process. I embraced it.

After that night, I couldn't care less what people said or thought about me. I was trying to live for God. I learned that just because a person thinks a certain way about you, that doesn't necessarily mean they are right about you. Who are they? Your opinion about yourself holds greater value than someone else's opinion about you. As long as my motives were pure and God was pleased with me, that was all that mattered. Of course, having a pastor with a pure heart watching over my soul made all the difference in this process.

Oftentimes, it's nothing personal against you with the church people; it's that the enemy wants to push you out the church. The folks don't realize that they are being used. When we experience church hurt, it is not always meant for us to leave. God sometimes wants to give us victory in it in order to help someone else that has to go through it. There are so many hurting people in the church that are waiting for you to show up and tell them how you got victory in your experience. Jesus and His disciples represented the church. Jesus told them that one would betray Him and the other would deny Him. He was letting us know what to expect.

> ***Now when the even was come, he sat down with the twelve. And as they did eat, he said, Verily I say unto you, that one of you shall betray me… Jesus said unto him, Verily I say unto thee, That this night, before the cock crow, thou shalt deny me thrice. (Matthew 26:20–21, 34, KJV)***

If Jesus had to experience this, then why shouldn't we have to? This is what goes on in the church because many individuals do not know what their purpose is. When we know what our purpose in life is, we don't have time for foolishness. The problem is that "church" can't teach people what their purpose is; only God can reveal that. However, most churchgoers do not have a personal relationship with God in order to find that out. Most churches focus on religion and do not even understand that religion can't take us where God is leading us. Jesus didn't say seek religion, but He said, "Seek first the Kingdom of God and His righteousness and all these things will be added unto you."

> ***"But seek ye first the kingdom of God, and his righteousness; and all these things shall be added unto you" (Matthew 6:33).***

When we learn to seek the Kingdom of God, then He will reveal the hidden things that man or this world could never show us.

Time went by and God had taken me to another level in ministry. When you are trying to live right and do the will of God, you have to understand that the enemy is going to come at you with all kinds of tactics. He will come at you harshly, may it be your marriage, your finances, your children, your health—whatever he uses, you must understand that it's all a part of the process of getting you to your destiny.

God gave me revelation of the mentality that he wanted to establish in me through that great deliverance that had taken place on that island. He took me to the book of Luke, where Jesus was on his way to the cross. The Bible says that there were some women following that bewailed and lamented him. In other words, they were crying and weeping. God showed me that there is a certain mentality that we as followers of Christ should have, even when we are going through our fiery tests and trials.

> ***"But Jesus, turning unto them said, "Daughters of Jerusalem, weep not for me, but weep for yourselves, and for your children" (Luke 23:28).***

In spite of Jesus's turmoil, He still forgot about Himself and encouraged somebody else, even as He was going to the cross. He knew what lay ahead of him. This is the mind-set that we have to adopt. This mind-set is crucial to a believer because you realize that it's not about you. It is about the will of God for your life. We will find ourselves in circumstances and situations where people look on us and see us going through it. They will see the scars, wounds, knives in our backs; however, it is all for the glory of God. There is a greater place to which God desires to take us, and the only way of getting to that place oftentimes is through suffering with Christ.

> ***"And if children, then heirs; heirs of God, and joint-heirs with Christ; if so be that we suffer with him, that we may be also glorified together. For I reckon that the suffering of this present time are not worthy to be compared with the glory that is to be revealed in us" Romans 8:17–18).***

Although we may suffer as believers, we are victorious. The glory of God that comes with the suffering is worth everything that we have to endure. So, it does not matter what people say or think about us when we are going through trials. When you have a "weep not for me" mentality, it takes you a long way. You realize that it is more important to decrease so that someone else can increase. You allow your fleshly man to die so that someone else's spirit man can live. Don't get caught up in trying to hide and cover up your tests and trials. Let people see you going through them because when God brings you out, everybody is going to know that the God you serve has surely delivered you. After Daniel was thrown into the lion's den, God delivered him. When the king saw this, he declared that the whole nation would serve his God.

> ***"I make a decree, That in every dominion of my kingdom men tremble and fear before the God of Daniel: for he is the living God, and steadfast forever, and his kingdom that which shall not be destroyed, and his dominion shall be even unto the end" (Daniel 6:26).***

Jesus knew that He would reign again. Even in enduring the cross, he knew that in three days, the glory of God would be revealed. He was focused on the ultimate outcome and not on his current situation. We have to focus on the ultimate outcome of our trials. There is always a greater picture. The devil's job is to cause us to lose focus on the ultimate outcome and become discouraged. If we become discouraged and walk away from the purpose and plan for our lives, then he wins, and so many people lose. One believer can affect the lives of many people. In this transition, we learned how to suffer for the glory of God. We learned how to hold our heads up high and look at the greater plan and purpose for our lives. Jesus was anointed for the task that was set before him, and he endured to the end.

> ***"Looking unto Jesus the author and finisher of our faith; who for the joy that was set before him endured the cross, despising the shame, and is set down at the right hand of the throne of God" (Hebrews 12:2).***

We must know that we have been anointed to go through whatever it is that we have to go through. If you find yourself going through a hard trial, you are anointed for the task. You just have to learn to trust and praise God in your going through. So the next time the enemy tries to make a fool or mockery out of you through your tests and trials, just remember Jesus on His way to the cross. Stand on the mountaintop and shout with the voice of triumph, "Weep not for me because I am anointed for the task!"

Chapter 8

It Had to Happen

One day, I was over at my grandmother's house during a family gathering. My nephew made a comment about my dad losing a lot of weight. He even said that my dad thought he might be sick. This took me by surprise. I had not paid any attention to the weight loss. Shortly after that, I found out that during a family reunion trip that I didn't attend, he had gotten really sick. So, I called him, and we talked for hours. I didn't even get to mention anything about him being sick because we were on the subject of God. We talked about nothing else except for how good God was. The irony was that my dad wasn't saved. He visited my church every now and then; however, before we got off the phone, I invited him to church. It was Saturday. He said, "You know what, baby, I think I will come to church tomorrow." Sure enough, he came.

This time it was different though. He had come to my church several times. He loved the bishop. However, he never came up for prayer during the altar call. This time, he came up for prayer. The bishop laid hands on him and prayed for him. He fell to the floor! He was lying on the floor. His body was moving as if he was trying to get up but couldn't. He was down there for a little while, and when he got up, he grabbed me saying, "Baby, God is real. He really is real. I tried to get up with all my might and couldn't get up. God is real." We talked on the phone that evening, and all we could talk about was his experience. It was a life-changing experience for him. He was so excited. He told me that he had a doctor's appointment that following day.

He found out at that appointment that he had fourth-stage cancer of the duodenum with metastasis to the liver, pancreas, and lungs. Wow! What a blow in the gut for us all. He was only fifty-five years old. However, my dad was amazing in all this. He took on a very positive attitude toward it all. Where do we go from here? The doctors were recommending chemotherapy. He started with natural herbs, which I thought were working great. The doctors were amazed that he was not in any pain, and he looked wonderful. I knew that it was God's grace on him. He started going to Bible Academy and church regularly.

Then one Bible study, he came and said that all hell was breaking loose in his home. He was so upset and stressed about what was going on. I thank God for the bishop. I asked him if he had a few minutes to counsel with my dad. He immediately said, "Yes." He met with him and, until this day, I don't know what they talked about. One thing I do know is that my dad came out of that office with a peace of mind. He thanked me for setting up the meeting. After that, I thought about backing off from visiting my dad and just call him on the phone because I didn't want to cause him any more problems in his home.

My dad's wife didn't care much for me. She was the same woman that came between my mom and dad. I accepted her in my life because I loved my dad. However, there was always an insecurity in her when it came to my dad's relationship with me. My dad and I were very close, and I later learned that she thought that I was trying to get my mom and dad back together. This was ridiculous! They were two adults. My mom didn't desire that at all. She just prayed for my dad and wanted him to get saved. With the chaos my dad was facing at home, I thought maybe I shouldn't visit for a while because I did not want to stress him. A certain individual forbade me to stop visiting because I wasn't a part of the problem. I was told that I didn't know how long my dad would be here and that it was all part of the enemy's plan to keep me from my dad. I just wanted to keep as much stress as possible off my dad, but I understood what they were saying.

My dad always called me his baby. He would always tell me how proud of me he was. He had the opportunity to hear me minister a couple of times, and he'd always say that I made his chest stick out. I went into prayer. I found myself struggling with logic and faith—what I knew versus what I believed. Being in the nursing field, I knew that liver and pancreatic cancer usually leads to death. I prayed to God to heal him and let this cup pass from him. I knew that it would take a miracle to change the prognosis. I kept my thoughts and feeling to myself and spoke faith. My brother had not spoken to my dad in a while because of a minor disagreement. However, while I was running a revival in Georgia, my dad and brother went out to dinner, and the forgiveness process was initiated between them. It was a little rocky at first; however, they were able to work through it and resolve their issues.

Shortly after that, I got the call that my dad had been rushed to the ER. When I got there, he was not able to talk. He was having seizure-like activities. After a CAT scan, we were told that the cancer had spread to his brain and that they needed to start radiation. The radiation was a success. He started chemotherapy shortly after. After starting the chemotherapy, he acquired pneumonia. Chemo kills the good cells as well as the bad cells, leaving the body's immune system weakened. I remember talking to him on the phone one night and asking him if he was coming to church on Sunday. He told me that he was going to go to my cousin's church because they were going to have communion, and he really wanted to have communion.

It was a Wednesday night, the last week in December, and New Year's Eve was that Friday night. We just happened to be having communion at our church New Year's Eve watch night service. I invited him out to watch night service. He had never been to a watch night service before. I told him that we were having communion that night. He was excited and said that he would come. New Year's night came, and I was in church. I walked out of one of the rear doors into the sanctuary and heard someone coughing really hard. When I looked up, I saw my dad. I didn't know that he was there already. However, when I laid eyes on him, I got butterflies in my stomach and ran to him. I asked him if he was okay. He told me yes. He looked different to me. He was slumped forward, and his skin was real dark. The service that night was good, and I got a chance to have communion with my dad for the first and—little did I know—the last time. I was blessed that night. I couldn't stop crying.

That Sunday, I called him after I got home from church to see if he went to my cousin's church. He told me that he didn't make it because he didn't feel well. We were so glad that he came to my church for watch night service for communion. I know that God created that opportunity for us to fellowship with communion together. My mom and I stopped by to see him. There was a moment when they had a few minutes alone, and my dad told her that he always wanted to tell her how sorry he was for hurting her. He told her that hurting her was the worst thing that he had ever done in his life. He also told her that when he heard that she was saved, that he knew that God would take care of her and that he hoped to be saved like her one day. My mom had been hurt deeply by their divorce. However, once she received Christ as her Lord and Savior, she never stopped praying for him. She had already forgiven him way before he asked her. You get true liberty when you release those who hurt you. Truth be told, many people who hurt others truly do not want to hurt the people they hurt; and oftentimes, they do it beyond their control. They often regret the mistakes they made. We all make terrible mistakes in our lives without the power of the Holy Spirit abiding in us.

Later that week later, I received a call that my dad had been rushed to the hospital. When I got there, he had on a partial rebreather mask. He was having difficulty breathing. He was so weak. I had to feed him. I stayed until visiting hours were over. The next morning, I got a call stating that my dad called his wife, saying that he was about to be intubated.

I picked up my sister and headed to the hospital. When we got there, they were running with him through the hall. I couldn't believe my eyes. They rushed him to ICU. It was Saturday. I never left the hospital until he made his transition on the following Monday, January 11, 2005.

This was a devastating time for us. My dad was gone at age fifty-six. He was diagnosed with cancer in August of 2004, and five months later, he was no longer with us. The hospital ICU was flooded with family members. Bishop was right there when he passed away. He has always been there when we needed him most. During the course of that week, I didn't say a whole lot. We were in revival that week. I had to minister. Bishop told me that I didn't have to if I didn't want to, but I did anyway, only because I knew that my dad was proud that I accepted my call as a minister, and he would not have wanted it any other way. I wanted to make him proud. I stepped back and let my uncles and his wife do what needed to be done.

During the course of my dad's relationship with his wife, I was accused of not liking her. This was so far from the truth, and I refused to spend a lot of time defending myself on that matter. My love for my dad surpassed any personal feelings that I had. I cared for anyone that he cared for.

The day of the funeral arrived. I was numb as we rode in the limousine to the church. When I got to the funeral, I kept hearing,

"Praise Me," in my spirit. I remember going to the restroom and pacing around in there. Again, I heard "Praise Me"; however, this time I heard loud and clear that. "If you don't praise Me now, you will get into a state of depression, and it will take a long time to shake it off." During the homegoing service, there was a space allowed for ministers. I felt bad that I had to take the opportunity to say something during this time; however, it was then or never. I got up and gave God praise for allowing my dad to walk around without pain.

I blessed God for the most important thing, and that was him giving his life to Christ the day before he found out what his illness was. I praised Him because my dad got his business in order before making his transition. He made amends with my mother and my brother. I testified that the enemy had tried for years to sever my brother's, sister's, and my relationship with our dad, but he was not successful. By the time I was through giving God praise, half the church was up in praise. Afterward, I had family members from my dad's side and his wife's side saying that they really needed to hear that. I blessed God to know that I was used as my dad's final mouthpiece. The Lord told me a long time ago that the enemy desires to shut my mouth. I know he does, but he is a liar.

The next day was rough. I began to pray and intercede for the family, especially his wife. I remember the pain when my dad left us, and I couldn't help but to feel bad for his wife because she was now experiencing the same type of pain. I tried calling her several times that day. I kept being told that she was not there or unavailable. Finally, I started to think that something was wrong. I called her daughter to find out if things were okay, and she told me that she was going to check for me. Shortly after that, I received a phone call from my dad's wife's sister. She asked me why I was calling. She said that it was over, he was gone. She was harsh and cold. She told me that I do not need to call there anymore. I was in awe. My exact words were, "God bless you," and I hung up the phone.

Sad to say, after that encounter with them, I had no further dealing with her. "God knows best" is what I say. You can't make someone like you, and you sure can't spend your life trying to convince them that you like them. It is only what is in a person that will come out. If it is not in a person to say or do a thing, they won't.

After my father passed away, I felt as though my security blanket was gone. Change had to occur. I needed to embrace this new place and move forward. It was necessary for my natural and spiritual survival. Consider the eagle, if you will. When it is time for the eagle to prepare the eaglet to learn to fly, which is a great change, the mother eagle takes the eaglet and tosses it out of the nest. The eaglet immediately jumps back in on instincts. So the next time the mother eagle tosses the eaglet out of the nest, she hurries and plucks up the feathers and leaves that was serving as a cushion and exposes the thorns. When the eaglet jumps back in the nest, the thorns stick it; and immediately, it jumps back out crying, squeaking, and probably wondering why its mother is doing this. The mother eagle knows and understands that this change is vital in order for her eaglet to survive in life.

After this process, the mother eagle takes the eagle and throws it off of the cliff. As the eaglet is falling to the ground, it is fearful and is again probably wondering why its mother has done this. However, before it reaches the bottom, the eagle comes and swoops it up on its back. It takes the eaglet to the landing. This process goes on until the eaglet learns how to fly. No matter what we go through in life, we must learn that it is a part of change. Change is needed in order for us to get to the place where God is trying to take us to. We might not understand everything that is going on at the time; however, we can understand that it is working for our good.

> ***"And we know that all things work together for good to them that love God, to them who are the called according to his purpose" (Romans 8:28).***

God wants us to trust Him no matter what is occurring in our lives. He wants us to surrender our total will to Him, trust Him, and praise Him. When we learn to do these three things, our will lines up with His will.

We have to understand that some things have to happen in order to push us into the position where God is taking us. Elijah was a great prophet of God that caused the whole nation of Israel to bow down before God and worship Him on Mount Carmel.

> ***And it came to pass at the time of the offering of the evening sacrifice, that Elijah the prophet came near, and said, LORD God of Abraham, Isaac, and of Israel, let it be known this day that thou art God in Israel, and that I am thy servant, and that I have done all these things at thy word. Hear me, O LORD, hear me, that this people may know that thou art the LORD God, and that thou hast turned their heart back again. Then the fire of the LORD fell, and consumed the burnt sacrifice, and the wood, and the stones, and the dust, and licked up the water that was in the trench. And when all the***

> ***people saw it, they fell on their faces: and they said, The LORD, he is the God; the LORD, he is the God. (1 Kings 18:36–40)***

However, Elijah ordered that all the false prophets of Baal be killed. They were enemies of God. This was a courageous thing. It is never popular to stand up against the odds in doing the will of God. The Bible says that when Jezebel found out what he had done to her prophets, she swore on her life to kill him. When Elijah heard this, he ran into the wilderness and sat under a tree, asking God to let him die.

> ***Then Jezebel sent a messenger unto Elijah, saying, So let the gods do to me, and more also, if I make not thy life as the life of one of them by tomorrow about this time. And when he saw that, he arose, and went for his life, and came to Beersheba, which belongeth to Judah, and left his servant there. But he himself went a day's journey into the wilderness, and came and sat down under a juniper tree: and he requested for himself that he might die; and***

> ***said, It is enough; now, O LORD, take away my life; for I am not better than my fathers. (1 Kings 19:2–4)***

Know that sometimes, in doing the will of God, you can become discouraged. However, God always has another plan. The enemy's job is to discourage us from doing the will of God in any way possible. He will do anything to try to get us to lose focus. God sent an angel to minister to Elijah, also giving him divine food and drink and told him to arise and eat because the journey before him was great.

> ***And as he lay and slept under a juniper tree, behold, then an angel touched him, and said unto him, Arise and eat. And he looked, and, behold, there was a cake baking on the coals, and a cruse of water at his head. And he did eat and drink, and laid him down again. And the angel of the LORD came again the second time, and touched him, and said, Arise and eat; because the journey is too great for thee. And he arose, and did eat and drink, and went in the strength of that meat forty days and***

***forty nights unto Horeb the mount of God.* (1 Kings 19:5–8)**

Our Christian journey is very long, and for those that have been called to ministry, the journey can also be lonely at times. Elijah had become depressed, even after just causing a whole nation to bow down and worship God. This serves as an example that no matter how far we go in our ministry, we are well capable of becoming discouraged and losing focus of God's will for our life. However, after the angel ministered to Elijah, he got up in his new strength and went up to Mount Horeb.

We must allow God to give us a new strength when we become discouraged. When he arrived at the top of Mount Horeb, God asked him what he was doing there. He wanted to know how Elijah would respond. Elijah told God that he was jealous for Him because the children of Israel had forsaken their covenants with Him, torn down their altars, killed His prophets, and seek even to kill Elijah himself. God told him to go stand out on the mount. In other words, he hadn't gotten the revelation yet. He needed to go a little farther. Sometimes, God tries to show us revelation through our trials; but oftentimes, we miss it because we focus more on the trials than on what it is we are supposed to get out of the trial. The Bible says that when Elijah went out on the mount, there was strong wind, an earthquake, a fire, and then a still small voice.

> ***And he said, Go forth, and stand upon the mount before the LORD. And, behold, the LORD passed by, and a great and strong wind rent the mountains, and brake in pieces the rocks before the LORD; but the LORD was not in the wind: and after the wind an earthquake; but the LORD was not in the earthquake: And after the earthquake a fire; but the LORD was not in the fire: and after the fire a still small voice. (1 Kings 19:11–12)***

Although there may be many strong winds that come in our lives that seem to tear and break things up, oftentimes, God is not in that. There may be what seem to be earthquakes that come and destroy some things and fires that come to burn things up, but God is oftentimes not in these things either. These are known distractions that are designed to get us to miss that still small voice where God is. God told Elijah that He had kings and prophets for him to anoint. He told him that there were seven thousand people that never even bowed down to or kissed Baal (the enemy). (See ***1 Kings 19:15–18***.)

God had given Elijah a greater revelation, a greater anointing, and a greater purpose. Know that the tests and trials that often lead us to a road of discouragement are often the ones that lead us to greatness, if we allow God access to minister to us. Some things have to happen, but after it all, there is a greater level that God will reveal.

Understand that there is a nation of people that is waiting for you. Your trials are not in vain. There are individuals that are waiting for you to show up with your testimony. You have to tell the world how God delivered you out of a horrible pit. Leaders, there are some folk that you have to go and anoint and appoint. The vision is greater than what you can see at the present time of your trials. The trials had to happen to prepare you for the greater work of God. God has chosen you for His glory, and when He brings you out with His mighty hand, no one can get the glory but Him.

> ***"Ye are my witnesses, saith the Lord, and my servant whom I have chosen: that ye may know and believe me, and understand that I am he: before me there was no God formed, neither shall there be after me" (Isaiah 43:10).***

If God's chosen aren't convinced of who He is and what He can do, then God's people are in trouble. So we have to go through the sifting process. When something is being sifted, it is put through a straining device. This process is designed to separate the fine particles from the coarse particles. It is designed for God to examine us and closely screen us. Unfortunately, this does not feel good, but it is necessary in order to become who God has called and chosen us to be. He puts His signature on His chosen. After the sifting process, then He gives us His seal of approval. This seal of approval validates and affirms the anointing on our life. Validation and affirmation are vital to those that are called out and chosen by God to do a great work because it gives authority to carry out the will of God! Do you understand now why it had to happen?

CHAPTER 9

Cast Down but Not Destroyed

Years went by. I had gone forward in life and ministry. The Lord spoke a word that I would not be in the church I was attending in the next few years. Not long after that, He spoke Tennessee. I didn't quite understand it all, but I have always been one to be as obedient to the voice of the Lord, as I know how. I just left it at that until I heard further from the Lord on it.

In 2011, I started working on my second degree in nursing when I decided to write a book. To make a long story short, I had written it and submitted it to my publisher. To my surprise, it was completed and ready to be released much sooner than I had anticipated. I had to make a decision to quit the program altogether or travel with my new book release. Well, needless to say, after I failed the nursing class by three points and being a 3.5 nursing student, I knew that I was to take the path of my book. So I did. I released it January 2012. I traveled with the book, doing book signings, speaking engagements, etc. It was truly a blessing. Many lives were blessed by the book. In March 2012, I had preached in a women's conference in Virginia and Georgia. We went into the enemy's territory and snatched folk out of witchcraft; many lives were changed, healed, and set free during that time. We saw the power of God move. We saw people healed and delivered. There was a young lady and her mom delivered out of witchcraft. I returned home and was back to work a couple days after. I received a call from my husband at that time, telling me that he lost his keys and may need me to pick him up after I left my last patient's house. I called him while walking out of my patient's home to see if he needed me to come. He said yes. He was upset, stating he traced all his steps but have no idea where his keys were. As I was pulling out of my patient's apartment building, I heard a voice very strongly say, "Stop and access you GPS." The ironic part about this was I knew where he worked. However, the voice was so strong and impressionable, I obeyed. I literally stopped in the middle of the road, which was a two lane-road, one lane each way. I put my foot on the brake, looked down, hit my GPS button, and looked back up. Where I would have been had I not stopped and accessed my GPS button was a side street in front of me with a stop sign. There was an SUV going about 80–90 mph that blew the stop sign! I yelled,

"JESUS!" Tears rolled down my face, and I was shaking because I knew what had just taken place. It was literally DIVINE intervention. I was still in the middle of the street, with one foot on the brake, shaking, crying, and praising God all at the same time. I was frozen. I could not move. Then right after that, there was a police car with no siren that came flying across, busting through the stop sign. driving just as fast as the SUV. It was a high-speed chase. I was so done. I knew that God had supernaturally intervened on my behalf. I praised God while crying and was overcome with emotions. I finally managed to get myself together and arrived to my destination. I told him what happened and told him that he would find his keys and that him losing them had nothing to do with him. God used it to save my life because if it had not been for the keys being lost, there would have been absolutely no reason for me to stop and access my GPS, and I would not be here to write this book. Glory to God. When I returned home, I walked in the restroom and turned the light on. I heard the Lord say to me, "I am He that is alive but was once dead. I hold the keys to hell and of death. I have given you the keys to hell and of death, whatsoever you bind on earth shall be bound in heaven and whatsoever you loose on earth shall be loosed in heaven."

My life was never the same after that. I began to see things in a different perspective and walk in a new authority that I couldn't explain, nor did I truly understand it. When God deals with you supernaturally, don't allow others to try to dumb it down. Don't try to explain what you don't have the answer to. Sometimes, you simply have to allow God to do what He is doing in you and be obedient while thriving in the midst of uncertainty. He let me know from that point on that I would be amongst the trailblazers, forerunners, and trendsetters. I realized that my life was not my own. I owed God my everything.

Then one Sunday morning after coming off the road from ministering, God told me that I was only to impart in others but not get involved with the affairs of the church, and to lie on the altar as He led me until He released me from that place. I did exactly that. My God…after months of lying on the altar when I wasn't on the road traveling, He released me; and when He did, my eyes were open to the kingdom of God, and the spirit of religion was broken off me! I didn't even know anything about either until revealed by the Holy Spirit Himself. I began to see things in a different light. I saw that the work of God was greater than the four walls of the church building. I had divine knowledge of the five ascension ministry without any man teaching me. God ministered to me from ***Ephesians 4:8–16***:

> ***Wherefore he saith, When he ascended up on high, he led captivity captive, and gave gifts***

unto men. Now that he ascended, what is it but that he also descended first into the lower parts of the earth? He that descended is the same also that ascended up far above all heavens, that he might fill all things.) And he gave some, apostles; and some, prophets; and some, evangelists; and some, pastors and teachers; For the perfecting of the saints, for the work of the ministry, for the edifying of the body of Christ: Till we all come in the unity of the faith, and of the knowledge of the Son of God, unto a perfect man, unto the measure of the stature of the fulness of Christ: That we henceforth be no more children, tossed to and fro, and carried about with every wind of doctrine, by the sleight of men, and cunning craftiness, whereby they lie in wait to deceive; But speaking the truth in love, may grow up into him in all things, which is the head, even Christ: From whom the whole body fitly joined together and compacted by that which every joint supplieth, according to the effectual working in the measure of every

part, maketh increase of the body unto the edifying of itself in love.

It was plain as day to me. The scripture was literally self-explanatory, but somehow, we have danced all around this chapter and took out what we wanted. This is why there has been no real dunamis power in the church as a whole because we are not operating in the fullness of Christ. We have not fully experienced His Kingdom. *HE* has placed a portion of Himself in us all, but in order to experience the fullness of Christ, we must all come together and operate together with all the gifts given to the church. He began to reveal His Kingdom to me because I began to seek Him in another place. I am a living witness that Holy Spirit can reveal all things. We just have to position ourselves to hear from Him. So many have taken away and added to the Holy Scriptures. This is why we don't see the dunamis power of God displayed often in the body of Christ. Ephesians 4:8 speaks of Jesus ascending, which meant this was after His resurrection. Then it says He gave gifts unto men. Verse 9 says he descended to the lower parts of the earth then above all heavens that all things might be fulfilled. He gave apostles, prophets, evangelists, pastors, and teachers. These are the fivefold ascension ministry gifts given to the church so that we may operate in unity and in the fullness of the power of our Christ. This is plain and simple, not deep. Now, of course, everyone is not called to the fivefold ministry. These gifts are a part of the government of God. Church is not a religion but a government. These gifts are appointed by God only and not man. However, man can consecrate you into these offices. There are many other gifts in the body of Christ.

> ***Now concerning spiritual gifts, brethren, I would not have you ignorant. Ye know that ye were Gentiles, carried away unto these dumb idols, even as ye were led. Wherefore I give you to understand, that no man speaking by the Spirit of God calleth Jesus accursed: and that no man can say that Jesus is the Lord, but by the Holy Ghost. Now there are diversities of gifts, but the same Spirit. And there are differences of administrations, but the same Lord. And there are diversities of operations, but it is the same God which worketh all in all. But the manifestation of the Spirit is given to every man to profit withal. For to one is given by the Spirit the word of wisdom; to another the word***

> ***of knowledge by the same Spirit; To another faith by the same Spirit; to another the gifts of healing by the same Spirit; To another the working of miracles; to another prophecy; to another discerning of spirits; to another divers kinds of tongues; to another the interpretation of tongues: But all these worketh that one and the selfsame Spirit, dividing to every man severally as he will. (1 Corinthians 12:1–11)***

So it is not about titles; we all have our own perspective places in the body of Christ. It was never designed for one person to run an entire church on his or her own and operate in all the ministry gifts alone. That is too much stress for one person. The church is not a religion; it is a government. In order to under the Kingdom of God, you must understand government. We are called to legislate God's kingdom in the earth realm, but this is not happening because we have gotten trapped in religion. We have gotten caught up in religious practices, which hide what is really within us and keeps us bound on the inside. We have become ignorant to the principles of God and refuse to get away from the religious practices and traditions of men, which Jesus did away with on the cross.

God have gifted us all. This is why many get lost, discouraged, and fall by the wayside right in the church. They are not being used in the capacity that God ordained for them, nor are they operating in the ministry gifts that they are called to. If we are not fulfilling our God-ordained purpose in life, we deteriorate spiritually, thus leaving us to deteriorate emotionally, mentally, and often physically.

Many have argued that there is no such thing as modern-day apostles and prophets. The argument has been that only the disciples that walked with Jesus are apostles. However, Paul, who was one of the greatest apostles that walked the earth, did not walk with Jesus but rather had a supernatural experience with Christ on the road to Damascus, and there were others.

> ***And Saul, yet breathing out threatenings and slaughter against the disciples of the Lord, went unto the high priest, And desired of him letters to Damascus to the synagogues, that if he found any of this way, whether they were men or women, he might bring them bound unto Jerusalem. And as he journeyed, he came near Damascus: and suddenly there shined round about him a light from heaven: And he fell to***

the earth, and heard a voice saying unto him, Saul, Saul, why persecutest thou me? And he said, Who art thou, Lord? And the Lord said, I am Jesus whom thou persecutest: it is hard for thee to kick against the pricks. And he trembling and astonished said, Lord, what wilt thou have me to do? And the Lord said unto him, Arise, and go into the city, and it shall be told thee what thou must do. And the men which journeyed with him stood speechless, hearing a voice, but seeing no man. And Saul arose from the earth; and when his eyes were opened, he saw no man: but they led him by the hand, and brought him into Damascus. And he was three days without sight, and neither did eat nor drink

And there was a certain disciple at Damascus, named Ananias; and to him said the Lord in a vision, Ananias. And he said, Behold, I am here, Lord. And the Lord said unto him, Arise, and go into the street which is called Straight, and inquire in the house of Judas for one called Saul, of Tarsus: for, behold, he prayeth, And hath seen in a vision a man named Ananias coming in, and putting his hand on him, that he might receive his sight. Then Ananias answered, Lord, I have heard by many of this man, how much evil he hath done to thy saints at Jerusalem: And here he hath authority from the chief priests to bind all that call on thy name. But the Lord said unto him, Go thy way: for he is a chosen vessel unto me, to bear my name before the Gentiles, and kings, and the children of Israel: For I will shew him how great things he must suffer for my name's sake. And Ananias went his way, and entered into the house; and putting his hands on him said, Brother Saul, the Lord, even Jesus, that appeared unto thee in the way as thou camest, hath sent me, that thou mightest receive thy sight, and be filled with the Holy Ghost. And immediately there fell from his eyes as it had been scales: and he received sight forthwith, and arose, and was baptized. And when he had

received meat, he was strengthened. Then was Saul certain days with the disciples which were at Damascus. (Acts 9:1–19)

Needless to say, there are prophets all through the Bible. The question should be asked, why are pastors, evangelists, and teachers accepted but not apostles and prophets? Let me answer. The enemy is afraid of them. Apostles and prophets lay the foundation of the church. An apostle can operate in all five ministry gifts. Together, the apostle and prophet can establish the work while God brings in the rest of the team. With this appendage in place, the hand of God can make a fist; and power against the rulers of darkness is released to restore, renew, establish, and regain dominion over the earth. Without the restoration of the office of apostle, or any one of the offices for that matter, the government of God is incomplete and fragmented. The anointing that is on their lives can restore an old house of God, or build a new one. The apostle is one of God's greatest weapons against religion and tradition, and in fact, all carnality. They insist on holiness and separation for the true church. So along with the prophets, they do not mind ripping up and tearing down the mess and mold that has misled and defiled the church for so long. They will defend truth and spiritual law; are not afraid of religious leaders, money, or power that come against them. Apostles, along with the prophets, have the gifting to understand the rhema word and so are instrumental in restoring truth, which has been lost or forgotten as the church went through the dark ages, and they will do so at all costs. They are quite unafraid to attack false doctrines and criticize man's tradition. Where traveling ministers in the past for the most part have been afraid to speak a truth that may offend the people, the latter-day apostle, like the early church, will tell it like it is, regardless of the consequences. This is the nature of God operating through the apostolic and prophetic people. The softness of the Lamb is evident to love and care for the flock of God, but the aggression and boldness of the Lion opposes the enemy. Apostles are aware and understand that the spirits that are operating through the complacent and lukewarm church today are no different from the spirits of the old church. These spirits cause people to have eyes but not see and ears that don't hear. There is a spiritual dullness. Then there are those who are so caught up in worldliness that they have no interest in the things of God at all. But you see, judgment cannot come to even those that have no love for truth without them first being given the opportunity to accept it or reject it. In other words, the apostles put the truth out there for all but do not expect everyone to eagerly hear or accept it. Some that they minister the word to will turn out to be whitewashed graves, a brood of vipers, ones that cannot hear God's words through their message just like Jesus said many of those in the early church were. He also said many years ago that this kind are not His sheep, so the Word is given to these for judgment only, but it must be given to appease the scripture in ***Matthew 24:14***:

> ***"And this gospel of the kingdom will be preached in all the world to all the nations, and then the end will come."***

So, along with God's prophets, the apostle's message is of the Kingdom to those they preach to. The two-edged sword is in their mouth as the truth cuts you off or bring you healing. Like Apostle Paul said,

> ***"But as we have been approved by God to be entrusted with the gospel, even so we speak, not as pleasing men, but God who tests our hearts" (1 Thessalonians 2:4–5).***

They are compelled to speak truth, the full gospel of the Kingdom, to mankind. This is the mark of God's true sent ones. He has never sent false doctrine or watered-down truth to His people through His messengers! The early apostles were severely threatened and told not to speak in the name of Jesus or teach any doctrine that was contrary to the religion and tradition of the day, but let's look at their response…

> ***"But Peter and the other apostles answered and said: "We ought to obey God rather than men" (Acts 5:29).***

It is with this same tenacity that truth is spoken through the apostles today. Apostles Peter and John, at another incidence where the religious leaders had forbidden them to speak, told those that opposed them, "Whether it is right in the sight of God to listen to you more than to God, you judge!" Jesus spoke only truth. He never diluted it, and His message was considered hard by those who liked their life the way it was and didn't favor change.

> ***"And He said, 'Therefore I have said to you that no one can come to Me unless it has been granted to him by My Father.' From that time many of His disciples went back and walked with Him no more" (John 6:65–66).***

So the approach of speaking straight, unadulterated truth is not new with God, only man. Even the wicked must be offered an opportunity to change.

> ***And He said to me: "Son of man, go to the house of Israel and speak with My words to them. "But the house of Israel will not listen to you, because they will not listen to Me; for all the house of Israel are impudent and hardhearted. 11 And go, get to the captives, to the children of your people, and speak to them and tell them, 'Thus says the Lord GOD,' whether they hear, or whether they refuse." (Ezek. 3:4, 7, 11)***

The church has become so carnal. We have gotten away from the place of the altar. It is nothing new. As we veer from the altar, we become more like the world, thus leaving the church in a position to be powerless. Abraham established covenant with God and built an altar. However, when a famine hit the land, he ventured toward Egypt, which represents the world. As he got closer to Egypt, he became fearful of man and asked his wife Sarah to lie and say that she was his sister so Pharaoh would not kill him and take her for his own wife because she was so beautiful. So they lied, but the Bible tells us that God brought a plague on Pharaoh's house. Pharaoh knew then that Abraham had lied and sent him away without killing him. However, the Bible says that Abraham went back to the place where he was at the beginning, which was the altar. The church has to get back to the altar. The church has to get back to prayer.

> ***And there was a famine in the land: and Abram went down into Egypt to sojourn there; for the famine was grievous in the land. And it came to pass, when he was come near to enter into Egypt, that he said unto Sarai his wife, Behold now, I know that thou art a fair woman to look upon: Therefore it shall come to pass, when the Egyptians shall see thee, that they shall say, This is his wife: and they will kill me, but they will save thee alive. Say, I pray thee, thou art my sister: that it may be well with me for thy sake; and my soul shall live because of thee. And it came to pass, that, when Abram was come into Egypt, the Egyptians beheld the woman that she was very fair. The princes also of Pharaoh saw***

her, and commended her before Pharaoh: and the woman was taken into Pharaoh's house. And he entreated Abram well for her sake: and he had sheep, and oxen, and he asses, and menservants, and maidservants, and she asses, and camels. And the LORD *plagued Pharaoh and his house with great plagues because of Sarai Abram's wife. And Pharaoh called Abram, and said, What is this that thou hast done unto me? why didst thou not tell me that she was thy wife? Why saidst thou, She is my sister? so I might have taken her to me to wife: now therefore behold thy wife, take her, and go thy way. And Pharaoh commanded his men concerning him: and they sent him away, and his wife, and all that he had.*

And Abram went up out of Egypt, he, and his wife, and all that he had, and Lot with him, into the south. And Abram was very rich in cattle, in silver, and in gold. And he went on his journeys from the south even to Bethel, unto the place where his tent had been at the

beginning, between Bethel and Hai; Unto the place of the altar, which he had made there at the first: and there Abram called on the name of the LORD. (Genesis 12:10–20, 13:1–4)

Because the church has gotten away from the altar, it has gotten caught up in religious ideology, legality, transition of men, and titles that we have missed the true purpose of the kingdom of God. We have stopped focusing on relationship with Christ and are more focused on the four walls of the church. Many have turned the church into a business. The church was never designed for this purpose. Our Christ did not die so that we would become so tied up in the four walls, the brick and mortar, of the church while souls are being lost. However, the enemy, the opposer, knows that there was no real power of deliverance in the Levitical priesthood style of ministry, so he has deceived many into thinking that they are operating according to God's will. Sadly, many are operating in error. The problem with this is that many hearts are pure; however, many will be lost, and many will not fulfill their God-ordained purpose because the church is not operating in the fullness of Christ, which is in the Kingdom of our God. The enemy is set out to deceive and oppress God's people since the beginning of time. If he can keep us from ever coming into the true knowledge of the kingdom of God, then he has accomplished that which he set out to do.

So after the Lord released me from the altar, the spirit of religion was broken off me. Holy Spirit birthed me in the Kingdom of God without the help of any man. Of course, there were many after that God used to cultivate what He had began in me. You owe it to yourself to pray and ask God to show you the truth concerning the Kingdom of God. The spirit of religion is an enemy to God. It keeps His people and church in spiritual bondage. We have put limits and restraints on God through religious ideologies and traditions of men. There is a dunamis power, a fire that God is wanting to burst forth in the earth. He has preserved for Himself a remnant of people who He will use to set the church a flame! He is gathering His remnant in this season. There are individuals that have been set forth in the earth who has been processed for restoring the glory back to the church. This remnant has had to endure so much, but God is raising them up and have gone before them to position them for the great work of His Kingdom. True breakthrough and deliverance is coming to the church. If I'm speaking to you, your tests, trials, and tribulations have not been in vain, but they have been positioning you for greatness. You might have been cast down, but definitely not forsaken. Your day is coming, and it will be glorious.

I will surely assemble, O Jacob, all of thee; I will surely gather the remnant of Israel; I will put them together as the sheep of Bozrah, as the flock in the midst of their fold: they shall make great noise by reason of the multitude of men. The breaker is come up before them: they have broken up, and have passed through the gate, and are gone out by it: and their king shall pass before them, and the LORD *on the head of them. (Micah 2:12–13)*

CHAPTER 10

Irreversible Process

November 2012, after touring all year long with my book, traveling the nation, ministering to the lost, seeing many lives transformed, saved, healed, set free, and delivered, the Lord spoke to me and said that I had been in the mist of a category 5 storm, but because of my obedience and faithfulness to him, He has had me in the eye of the storm, and I had not felt the effects of it. He said now I must come out and face the reality of what has hit me. Two months later, he revealed to me that my husband at that time of seventeen years was in an affair. I asked him, and he confessed. I did not ask him much about the affair. I just asked that he had nothing to do with her until we figure out what we were going to do. He agreed. Needless to say, the phone record showed that immediately after our conversation, he was on the phone with her and thereafter. The reality is after seeing him in a backslidden state for over a year,

I was still surprised that he had actually gone that far. I was disappointed and hurt. My true hurt was for my children. I knew I would be okay. I'd remember all the pain that I endured as a teenager having parents that went through this same ordeal.

Whenever anyone is out of the will and safety of God, they yield themselves to the enemy. This puts us in a place to destroy ourselves, our family, and anyone else. To be honest, I believe I was more hurt at the fact we were pillars in the church and we were supposed to be examples in the body of Christ. This type of behavior was becoming the norm in the church. I was upset that I was made another statistic and not by choice. The Bible says that we are surrounded by many clouds of witnesses. When professing Christ, our lifestyle should serve as a witness to others that we are representation of Christ.

> ***"Wherefore seeing we also are compassed about with so great a cloud of witnesses, let us lay aside every weight, and the sin which doth so easily beset us, and let us run with patience the race that is set before us" (Hebrews 12:1).***

At this point, I simply had to pursue the presence of God for direction. My prayer was that God's will be done and that my children came through this unscathed. Covenant is what many individuals who truly love God stay in a broken marriage for. I believed in waiting for God, and if He chose not to restore, I would be released through breaking of covenant by infidelity or abandonment according to the word of God.

God had revealed to me in that time that my season in the Michigan region was up and the time to pursue Tennessee was upon me. He gave me specific instructions. The first was to apply for jobs in Tennessee. I had applied two years ago just to see what kind of feedback I would get, and I got nothing. However, when I did it this time, I received multiple feedback and was able to set up interviews within a week. March of 2013, God told me to put my house on the market. I was leery of doing so because it needed a lot of work, including a roof. However, I was obedient, and within a week, I had a family knock on the door and offer me cash. It was sold within a month. I had gone to Tennessee on an interview and was hired on the spot. The only thing I didn't have was a home. I went to a conference in Virginia and happened to meet a couple in ministry who happened to live in the city I was looking to move in. They were beautiful, loving people; and after sharing my story, they insisted that I come stay with them when I came back to find a home, and I did just that. In two days, the Lord used them to find me a beautiful home.

God had given me favor with the landlord. I needed a quick commitment because my mother was having surgery after being diagnosed with cancer, and I had to be back in Michigan for that then return to start work in Tennessee a week later. God worked it all out. When we are moving according to God's will, the path is already paved. We just have to move…I went back to Michigan for my mom's surgery, and it was a success. The doctor said he removed all the cancer and she did not need chemo or radiation. Praise God!

Prior to moving, my husband told me that he did not want to lose his family. I told him that was between him and God. I moved to Tennessee. My boys had to stay and finish school but would come down a month later. They all came and joined me in Tennessee, including my mom. She told me that God told her that I would need her. The boys absolutely loved it. God had told me that around the time we moved to Tennessee, the twins would be in eighth grade and my baby in fifth grade; and sure enough, when I paid attention to it, they were surely in those grades. My husband at that time became a very angry and bitter man. He was so cold toward me. You would have thought I was the one who had the affair. My mother, children, and others were witnesses to this and also witnesses to the fact that I walked with pure humility during this process. Despite how he treated me, I cooked, cleaned, spoke to him with respect, and maintained my integrity and character gracefully. He was gone a lot, and the times he was at the house, he was bitter. One day, I was up in my closet crying and asking God, "Why is he here?" I did not want my children to see what was going on because all they had known before was us appearing well. He slept in a different room from the time he came. While I was in the closet praying, God spoke to me saying, *"Get your emotions under subjection. Am I not the same God that delivered you in Tennessee? If I delivered you in Michigan, I will deliver you in Tennessee. Now get up and get your emotions under subjection. There is a set time that I have given him, and in that set time, I will deliver you."* I immediately got up and began to praise God. I heard that loud and clear and without doubt that He would do just what He said He would do. At this point in my life, I chose to allow God to be God and wait patiently for Him to move on my behalf.

It is imperative that when we have been hurt or broken, that we seek God in a whole other place than what we have been accustomed to. You must be quick to forgive those who have violated or betrayed or you at risk for harboring bitterness, which can destroy your life. As I look back on the years prior, I can see how God prepared me on the altar for this great shift that was taking place in my life. Understand that God always prepares us for the next journey in our lives. This is why obedience to Him is so important.

One week I was at work, and I ran into another nurse in the supply room. She and I were talking, and she started crying. I distinctly recall her saying to me, "I just want my mother to be proud of me." I ministered to her, and the Lord blessed her. A few weeks later, she sent me message saying that the Lord laid it upon her heart to invite me to a conference being held in Smyrna, Tennessee. The irony of this was that the week of the conference, I was going to be home all by myself because my mom was going to Atlanta with a friend, and the boys were going to Michigan along with their father. God told me to go on a fast this particular week. He told me that I would be receiving a rhema word from Him.

The day of the conference came. I was so excited. I went with great expectation of a rhema word straight from the throne room of heaven. I arrived at the church early. It was a small church in downtown Smyrna. There were just a few people there when I arrived. The usher placed me on the very last row of the church. I did not understand that. Then I thought well, maybe she was reserving for other guests. The young lady who invited me arrived. She asked why was I sitting so far back, and I told her that was where they placed me. So I asked the usher if it was okay to sit up closer, and she pointed directly to the row in front of us. Our thinking was we might as well stay right where we were. So we did. While I was sitting there,

I noticed that they were having problems with their sound system. So they ended up having to pin the microphone to the pulpit, which meant when the speaker was up, she would not be able to move out of the pulpit.

The time came to introduce the guest speaker. I heard this angelic music playing as the evangelist introduced her. This was so unusual. While the evangelist was reading her biography, she had not come out. I recall hearing all the great things she had done in ministry and how she was connected to some pioneers in the gospel. If I may be honest, I was saying to myself, "Wow you mean a person of this caliber would come to a small-town church like this. She was from Texas." Well, she came from behind the wall in the pulpit, and I saw the glory of the Lord all over this woman. You could tell that this was someone who had been in the presence of the Lord. She shared a powerful testimony of how God have delivered her from drugs, death on so many occasions, polio disease, and so much more. Her testimony was amazing. She also said that she was recently married and was actually on her honeymoon when the Lord told her that she had a 911 case in Tennessee. She said that her husband had worked with her for years in ministry before they were married and understood her sensitivity to the call of God on her life. I was amazed. She ministered a great word, but I recall saying, "Lord, where is the rhema word?" She spoke in the lives of a few people who was up front. Remember, she could not come out of the pulpit because of the sound system issue. I was sitting all the way to the back. I couldn't help but to look around and see that the church was not even full and said we could have gotten closer. However, I tried not to allow that to distract me. At one point, she asked the evangelist who introduced her what time did she have to end, and they told her 10:00 p.m. She then asked what time it was, and it was ten thirty. So she apologized and wrapped it up. She said a generic prayer over everyone and closed out the service. I said, "Lord, that was a good word but I didn't receive a rhema word."

The young lady and I left, and they began to close everything down so fast. I truly have never seen anything like that in my life. We were standing by the young lady's car, talking. It was after 11:00 p.m. The next thing I know, the evangelist who introduced the speaker came running up to us, thanking us for coming. Then she looked and said, "There is Prophetess! Would you like to meet her?" We walked over to her. As I approached her, she looked at me and took a few steps back, shaking her head, and said to me, "Woman of God, you do not have any idea of the call of God that is on your life." She began to speak prophetically concerning the things that God has set before me. I was so done. She said to the evangelist that I was the 911 case that God sent her to. She went to say that there was a David in my life that has rejected God, and because he rejected God, God has rejected him. This lady knew nothing about me. Then she looked at the young lady who was with me and said to her, "You have been saying, 'I just want my mother to be proud of me.'" I almost fell out. This is exactly what she had recently said to me in that supply room. She went on to speak into her life, and the young lady was sobbing and crying out loud. When I looked up, we were the only four on the street. It was late. The church had closed up, and everyone had gone home. A train came by, and it masked the sound of the young lady crying aloud. The woman of God looked at me and said, "This is the type of deliverance ministry that God is calling you to. You will just speak a word, and folk will get delivered." She spoke many things concerning what the Lord would have her to share with me. I was truly blessed of the Lord that night. I got my rhema word from God. He sent His prophet all the way from Texas in the midst of her honeymoon to let me know that I matter to Him. Don't you know that God will not leave you or forsake you? No matter what we go through in life, God will be with you when you need Him the most.

That food took me in the strength of the Lord for a long time. I knew that no matter what was going on in my life, God already had a plan. I just had to be faithful to Him and wait till His plan manifested in my life. There is a process that is irreversible. It can't be stopped because it is needed to push up into God's divine position. It is all in the embracing of the process that determines our length and outcome.

Over a year had passed. One evening I walked past the room that my husband at that time slept in, and I heard the Holy Spirit say, "Go in and sleep." So I did. Around three in the morning, I had a vision of the entire room being infested with worms and snakes. I began a warfare, and when I came out of it, God revealed to me the presence of evil and infestation. He said that the worms represented that the problem in my home was greater than it appeared, and the snakes represented the presence of evil was in operation. He said He has kept my children and I covered thus far, but I could no longer continue to allow this to go on in my home, or else, we would eventually be overcome by this evil. I went to him and shared with him what God had shown me. He told me that he would leave. I was grateful that he had finally made a decision that he should have made a long time ago. He eventually made a decision to move back to Michigan. We divorced, and it was well in my soul that God released me.

Sometimes, our process in life is not always what we expect; however, when we learn to trust God and lean not to our own understanding, He is faithful to direct our paths.

"Trust in the LORD with all thine heart; and lean not unto thine own understanding. In all thy ways acknowledge him, and he shall direct thy paths. Be not wise in thine own eyes: fear the LORD, and depart from evil. It shall be health to thy navel, and marrow to thy bones" (Proverbs 3:3–7).

I had gotten to a place of peace in the midst of what I had to endure. There was a time where God told me that I would be as Daniel in the lion den and my children would be as the three Hebrew boys in the fiery furnace. He said that He would deliver us in the midst of it all, and we would come out just as they did. He did just that.

By the time we divorced, I had not been touched by him for over three years. Single people and those of you who are going through the same type of situation, you can be kept by God if you want to be kept. You can remain pure and maintain your good standing in Christ if you trust God and lean not on your emotions or fleshly desires. There was a time, at one point in that situation, I had asked God about that, and He told me that He would not allow him to contaminate my spirit. Consider it a blessing if you are in a situation where your spouse is unfaithful and will not touch you. Many spouses will still be intimate with their spouse while sleeping around with others. This can create an even bigger mess. I praise God for keeping and covering me. Hallelujah! I am a nurse by profession and know of situations where spouses have contracted incurable diseases by their unfaithful spouse.

I had come to a place in my life where I was content with being by myself. I even told God that if it meant me being single the rest of my life, raising my boys, and doing ministry, then so be it. I had gotten to a place of learning who I was a woman, and I enjoyed being me. God loved me. He made me feel so favored and special just like a good father does. He ministered to me. He told me anyone who is not content with being single and don't have a mind-set that never being married may be an option for them is not ready for marriage anyway, especially women. He says there will come a time where the male population will become so scarce that there would be an average of seven women for each surviving male.

> ***"And in that day seven women shall take hold of one man, saying, We will eat our own bread, and wear our own apparel: only let us be***

> ***called by thy name, to take away our reproach" (Isaiah 4:1).***

He also said reminded me that He said that it was not good for the man to be alone. He did not say it was not good for woman to be alone, and that He said when a man finds a wife, he finds a good thing and obtains favor from Him.

> ***"And the LORD God said, It is not good that the man should be alone; I will make him an help meet for him" (Genesis 2:18).***
>
> ***"Whoso findeth a wife findeth a good thing, and obtaineth favour of the LORD" (Proverbs 18:22).***

I truly understood the importance of being content in singleness because if you are not, the enemy would use your discontentment as a distraction from your purpose. I have known many women who get up daily with a focus on when their husband is coming and little focus on their purpose in life. When we begin to focus on our purpose in life, delight ourselves in the way of the Lord, and focus less on our personal desires, then will we see our desires become fulfilled.

"Delight thyself also in the LORD; and he shall give thee the desires of thine heart" (Psalm 37:4).

I am a living witness! One night, I had a vision. My teenage sweetheart showed up on my doorstep here in Tennessee. Yep! I said it…my teenage sweetheart; that young man that I was crazy about but had to part from—yes, him. It was a quick, sharp vision. He showed up on my doorstep, and the Lord said, "I've given him a Joseph experience." That was the vision. I woke up and asked, "Wow, what was that about?" The last time I had seen or heard from him was over ten years ago when I went to visit him as mentioned before. Now the ironic part to all this was two days later, his mom called out of the blue. Needless to say, we connected after that. When I spoke to him, he told me that he had been praying for me for years. He had been asking God to cover and keep me protected. He said that he had been praying that God would allow him a chance to make things right with me and to show me his heart toward me. He also prayed that God would bring me back into his life one day. He said that God showed him that I was handpicked just for him, but we had to go our separate ways so that we could become what we needed to become for God and each other. I felt as though I owed it to myself to find out if this man was truly my soul mate, the man that God created me for.

I began to pray and ask God, "Was this real?" Lord knows I don't play when it comes to my life, my children, and my walk with Christ. This was a hidden desire. He was not my first boyfriend, but he was my first love, and that place in my heart never left. I've loved, but he was the only man that I was ever truly "in" love with. I asked, "God can this be real?" My real concern was if his relationship with God real. You know we have all heard about many individuals going to prison and finding God, but the relationship only goes are far as they are in there. I don't take chances with my salvation or my life. However, the reality is that there are individuals that never saw a day in prison who confess Christ and live a life of total sin and disgrace. So I consulted the Lord about it. He is omniscient and omnipresent, all knowing and all seeing, everywhere at the same time.

Then one day I was working and I was not feeling well. I see patients in their homes, and I decided because I was not feeling well, that I would only see a few patients then go home early. Then I noticed a patient showed up on my schedule that we had discharged from our agency a few months earlier. I called my supervisor to inquire, and she said just go ahead and see her anyway. I thought this was very unusual. I really wasn't feeling well and really didn't feel like going, but it was heavy in my spirit to see her that day instead of moving her to the next day. The Bible declares that the steps of a good man are ordered by the Lord.

> ***"The steps of a good man are ordered by the LORD: and he delighteth in his way" (Psalm 37:23).***

So I set up the visit and went by there. When I got there, a gentleman walked out of the back. He was very pleasant. He offered me coffee, and I declined while sitting at the kitchen table with my patient. The gentleman kindly told my patient that he would be back shortly and left. After he left, my patient looked out the window to see if was gone and said, "Do you see that man right there?" I said, "Yes." She said, "That man just did thirty years in prison." She went on to say a few times that I just had to know him before he went in. She said that he has become an awesome Man of God and that he is not the same the man that he was when he went in. She appeared astonished. She said he prays several times a day, he studies his Bible on a regular basis, and goes to the shelter daily to minister to the homeless people. She kept saying, "You just had to know him before he went in." She said he was not the same man that he used to be. She said they used to fight and almost half killed each other, but God saved him while he was in prison. She kept saying, "God brought us full circle." When she said that, I got goose bumps all over my body and realized that I was no longer feeling sick. She told me that he would not touch her in a sexual way because they were not married. She laughed and said she tried to throw on her lingerie, but he still would not touch her in that way. I knew that Lord was speaking to me. I went home, and later, the Holy Spirit ministered to me and told me that He has brought us full circle. He told me that Shawn has had a Joseph's experience and thought He has brought us full circle for the purpose of His glory. He told me that I was the only woman that could receive him in this season of his life, and it couldn't just be any woman. I had been handpicked and prepared for him.

Years ago, I released a word that God would save many men and women in prison and release them with anointing that is like no other. They would stand flatfooted and not compromise the gospel of the kingdom. Little did I know that I was ministering to myself. Now please do not get me wrong. I am in no way advocating going out and getting someone in prison. You have to be truly led by the Spirit of God just as you have to be with anyone that you believe is your soul mate. I say *truly* because many individuals believe that they are being led by the Spirit of God on many occasions when they are simply being led by their soul man, which consists of the mind, emotions, and self- will. Many are led away by their own lusts.

> ***"Having a form of godliness, but denying the power thereof: from such turn away. For of this sort are they which creep into houses, and lead captive silly women laden with sins, led away with divers lusts" (1 Timothy 3:5–6).***

Your life is too precious and your salvation is too serious to take chances. You have to pray, fast, and live a life of consecration in order to keep yourself in a position to hear clearly from our Heavenly Father.

> ***My sheep hear my voice, and I know them, and they follow me: And I give unto them eternal life; and they shall never perish, neither shall any man pluck them out of my hand. My Father, which gave them me, is greater than all; and no man is able to pluck them out of my Father's hand. I and my Father are one. (John 10:28–30)***

There are many husbands and wives that are on the backside of the mountain in places such as prisons, crack houses, strip clubs, etc. Many are being hidden from the spirit of religion. Religion has contaminated so many Christians. When God save those individuals from those hard places, there will be such a powerful, no-nonsense anointing upon their lives, and many will be saved through them. When you are about your Heavenly Father's business and not worried about a spouse, little do you know He's cleaning them up while preparing you for them. God is a God that operates in timing and in seasons. It is imperative that as child as the Most High God, you always know what season God has you in so that the enemy do not have you going around a mountain longer than you are supposed to.

April of 2015, just a few months later, I was driving up the road, and I heard the voice of the Lord say, "Celebrate you." I asked out loud, "Celebrate me?" God said, "Celebrate you!" He said that the devil is set out to destroy me but because of my faithfulness and obedience to Him, the devil could not do what he desired to do to me. He quickly took me down memory lane of all the things that I encountered in life that should have destroyed me, the very same things that many have either gotten caught up on drugs, became alcoholics, or even committed suicide for, but God kept me. Hallelujah! I began to praise God right there while driving. There are times when we go through things in life that may seem devastating, unfair, defeating; however, we must always remember that Jesus went through for us, and He was without sin or fault in anything. We are identified with Christ through suffering. However, when we suffer with Him, we will also reign with Him.

"If we suffer, we shall also reign with him: if we deny him, he also will deny us" (2 Timothy 2:12).

The next month, I saw Shawn for the first time in ten years. He cried just like he did ten years earlier when I saw him. He couldn't control his tears. He could not believe that it was me, and yet this time, I was free. He reminded me that he had been asking God to cover and keep me protected. He said that he had been praying that God would allow him a chance to make things right with me and to show me his heart toward me. He also prayed that God would bring me back into his life. It was a very emotional gathering. Over the next year and a half, we prayed, talked, cried, studied scriptures over the phone. He was in Michigan. I was in Tennessee. This man ministered to me on so many levels. He didn't feed my emotions, but he fed my spirit man. He became my best friend. We could talk about anything. This was what I had been waiting for. I always had to be the strong one. So many people relied on me and counted on me for everything. If I didn't do a thing or think about a thing, things would not get done or get taken care of. I carried so much unimaginable weight on me it wasn't even funny. It was nothing but God's grace that carried me through the years and kept me sane. Literally, that is the truth. As a matter of fact, I recall a time when I looked by over my first marriage and asked God how in the world did I carry the weight that I did, and God told me that it was His grace and told me that I don't have that same grace to endure that again. The reality is we don't want to do anything without God's grace upon us.

Shawn had asked me to marry him during that period. I told him yes! I took him to several of my spiritual mentors for counsel. They all fell in love with him right away. We received their blessings and prayers. It is imperative to take the individual that you believe is your husband or wife to your spiritual leaders and/or mentors. Their blessings count, and prayers are essential to your future. This also will disrupt any plot or plan of the enemy to trip you up.

We planned our wedding together. We worked together in picking out everything. He is a hardworking man. He paid for just about everything on the wedding. We chose our high school prom colors. It was so beautiful. We were married on May 29, 2016. Praise the Lord.

He transitioned to Tennessee. I'll tell you what. We serve an amazing God. I liken myself to a woman of great faith. I have seen God do great things in my life. I have yet to tell it all. However, God went way in the depth of His bag of surprises and got me good with this one. I never saw this coming. We love each other so much. The love is the type of love that God ordained for a husband and wife. He cares for me like I always imagined I like to be cared for. He is so thoughtful. He does everything with me in mine. He loves God and His people. He is a leader and not a follower. He had a plan and was determined to follow his plan. That is a man. I know that he is a praying man because after twenty-three years of praying in prison, God gave him one of His best. Yes, I am one of God's best, and he agrees. As a matter of fact, to him, I am God's best, and that's the way it should be. Together we have been able to accomplish so much. We look forward to the ministry that God has set before us. We both look at each other and stand in awe at what the Lord has done. It is marvelous in our sight.

Yes, we have had some challenges. We have had to deal with jealousy and envy, ups and downs, but we chose to walk in love. We chose to live life God's way and not man's way. This is the best way of life. God has kept His word concerning us. He said that he would restore the years that the locust, cankerworm, and palmerworms have eaten up.

"And I will restore to you the years that the locust hath eaten, the cankerworm, and the caterpillar, and the palmerworm, my great army which I sent among you" (Joel 2:25).

In other words, what the devil meant for evil, God will turn around for our good. See, the devil sought out to destroy the both of us, but God had another plan. Hallelujah! Don't despise your process, baby. We have a great big God that says if you just trust Him, he will deliver you and place your life on track. It will be as though you never missed a beat. Glory to God! The half has yet been told... But God!

I'll tell you I was truly surprised of the reactions that I received from some individuals who say they are Christians when they found out that I was marrying my teenage sweetheart. They acted as if I had committed a crime because of our past. God showed us in this that the average-confessed believer, including many that are in ministry, do not believe in the power of God's true deliverance. Many go to church week after week, month after month, year after year, decade after decade; shout, praise, sit under the word; go through religious rituals; confess this and that but still deny the power thereof in Christ to deliver. This means that many confessed believers truly don't believe, which means they lack in their faith. It is impossible to please God without having faith because faith is believing. As believers of Christ, we believe that God himself came down from glory, wrapped Himself in flesh, was born of a virgin, through the law of nature became His own Son who was the Christ, died on the cross for the remissions of our sins, being known as the last blood sacrifice, arose three days later with all power in His hands, sent His spirit to dwell in us and give us power over the powers and rulers of darkness in the earth, and is now sitting on the right hand of God. This means that as long as we believe, the same power that was in Jesus is the same power that is in us now. So, no matter what we used to be or how much mess we were caught up in, we can be delivered by the power of the blood of our wonderful Savior Jesus Christ. Amen!

> ***"But without faith it is impossible to please him: for he that cometh to God must believe that he is, and that he is a rewarder of them that diligently seek him" (Hebrews 11:6).***

Let me say this: so what if people talk about you, look down on you, lie on you or think bad about you? It is what God has to say about you, how God sees you and think about you that truly matters. You have to walk in love, live holy, and make sure that the ugly things being said are not true. I have come to find out that most people that call themselves saved are messier than most people in the world. Many look for you to fall or look for opportunities to talk about you or look down on you rather than pray for you to make it or recover from hurt and brokenness. It is a sad reality, but I have learned to love God, love me, and love everyone in spite of it all. God has been so amazingly good to me, so I don't have time for hate, bitterness, or resentment in my heart. God revealed the true hearts of people to me during my process. It was so sad and disappointing. However, I am glad to know the truth. Now I stand in the gap and pray for those that I know are in need of true deliverance. God looks upon the heart of man. We tend to deceive ourselves, but God knows and sees all and deals with us all accordingly.

> ***"The heart is deceitful above all things, and desperately wicked: who can know it? I the LORD search the heart, I try the reins, even to give every man according to his ways, and according to the fruit of his doings" (Jeremiah 17:9–10).***

The Lord has told us that the second half of our lives will be blessed. We trust and believe Him! Hallelujah! I never knew love like this before. I've only imagined it, but God!

> ***"Many sorrows shall be to the wicked: but he that trusteth in the LORD, mercy shall compass him about" (Psalm 32:10).***

To God be the Glory for our lives. May He forever have His way in us.

Chapter 11

Shifted into Purpose

God can use any situation to shift us into our purpose. That is what He created us for—His purpose and His glory. We are created to legislate His Kingdom in the earth and glorify our Heavenly King. Our lives were set up to give God glory.

> ***"Even every one that is called by my name: for I have created him for my glory, I have formed him; yea, I have made him" (Isaiah 43:7).***

To *"set up"* is to put in readiness or adjustment for operation; to assemble and erect for position. Oftentimes, we fail to see the greater picture in the midst of our tribulations, and unfortunately, glory is often birthed through our pain. When a woman travail in labor, her mind is focused on the pain; however, the moment she delivers, the glory of the child supersedes the pain. There is a glory that God desires to take us to. I am a living witness.

I realize that every test, trial, and tribulation that I have endured over the years was pushing me into the position that God has me in today. He desires to manifest His glory in human form. God has positioned me to share my story with the nations and to let them know that He is a deliverer and a wonderful Savior. I don't have to wonder if He can deliver. I know that He can deliver.

> ***"Yea, before the day was I am he; and there is none that can deliver out of my hand: I will work, and who shall let it?" (Isaiah 43:13).***

God is saying that He will do the work in us. We just have to let Him do it. I have made up in my mind and spirit that I will allow God to do the work in me, which He has started.

I have had firsthand experience. Through these processes, I have learned to trust God and seek Him. As long as God can get the glory out of our lives, then our purpose is being fulfilled.

> ***"That the trial of your faith, being much more precious than of gold that perisheth, though it***

be tried with fire, might be found unto praise and honour and glory at the appearing of Jesus Christ" (1 Peter 1:7).

Understand that God's glory is revealed in us when people can look on us and see Him. It is so important that we seek God on a regular basis. There is a preparation period that we who are called into greatness have to go through. Salvation is greatness. Once we realize that everything we go through is positioning us for purpose, we must learn to press beyond the thorns of distraction in our life, as the Apostle Paul did.

And lest I should be exalted above measure through the abundance of the revelations, there was given to me a thorn in the flesh, the messenger of Satan to buffet me, lest I should be exalted above measure. For this thing I besought the Lord thrice, that it might depart from me. And he said unto me, My grace is sufficient for thee: for my strength is made perfect in weakness. Most gladly therefore will I rather glory in my infirmities, that the power

> ***of Christ may rest upon me. Therefore I take pleasure in infirmities, in reproaches, in necessities, in persecutions, in distresses for Christ's sake: for when I am weak, then am I strong. (2 Corinthians 12:7–10)***

The Bible never tells us what Paul's thorn was, letting us know that a thorn can be anything that causes pain or affliction. The most important thing for Paul was that the anointing and the power of God rest on him. So, if this meant that he had to suffer for it, then so be it. He learned to glorify in his afflictions. He learned to press beyond the thorns of distractions. There is greatness on the other side of our distractions, and the enemy knows this.

Distraction is a diversion from an original focus—anything that compels attention or creates extreme mental or emotional disturbance, obsession. The enemy will literally set up roadblocks in your life to hinder your progress. I had one particular thorn in my flesh in my early years that I can think. The first time it came, I asked God to let the cup pass from me, and it went away. This happened several times. It would come and go. The last time it came, and I prayed that God would let it pass, and He told me that He would not remove it because this time, it was getting ready to push me into my destiny. I literally saw God use this thing to catapult me into my destiny. No one said it would be easy, but it is certainly worth it.

I need you to consider the eagle again. It can see over five hundred kilometers away, and when it puts its eye on his prey, it never loses focus of it. No matter what distractions or obstacles come, it always keeps its eye on that prey until it gets it. We can't afford to lose focus on the vision and plan of God for our lives.

Moses was called unto greatness. He was called to lead the children of Israel out Egypt. However, he led them to the Promised Land, but he was not able to enter in himself. This was because he failed to press beyond the thorns of distraction, which was the rebellion of the children of Israel. His frustration and irritation with the children of Israel distracted him from obeying God. God had given him specific orders to carry out, but he was so angry and frustrated with the people that he did not do as God had specified.

> ***And Moses took the rod from before the LORD, as he commanded him. And Moses and Aaron gathered the congregation together before the rock, and he said unto them, Hear now, ye rebels; must we fetch you water out of this rock? And Moses lifted up his hand, and with his rod***

> ***he smote the rock twice: and the water came out abundantly, and the congregation drank, and their beasts also. And the LORD spake unto Moses and Aaron, Because ye believed me not, to sanctify me in the eyes of the children of Israel, therefore ye shall not bring this congregation into the land which I have given them. (Numbers 20:9–12)***

Anything that clouds our mind and overrides the orders of God serves as a distraction. We have to be so careful not to let the frustration of our trials keep us from getting to the place of glory that God has purposed for us. It is vital to our destiny that we seek after God's purpose and plan for our lives.

One night, I was in my study and found myself in Proverbs 31. One verse leaped out to my spirit.

> ***"Many daughters have done virtuously, but thou excellest them all" (Proverbs 31:29).***

He told me that He was concerned about those who will seek after His purpose and plan for their lives. He said that many have done well, many have done excellently, many have done righteously, but the ones that excel are the ones that seek after His purpose for their lives. They are the ones that find purpose because when you seek after God's divine purpose for your life, you end up walking in your destiny.

Destiny is an inevitable or necessary fate to which a particular person or thing is destined. It is the predetermined and unstoppable course of events considered as something beyond the power or control of man.

We must pursue God. To *pursue* is to follow in order to overtake or capture, to employ measures to obtain or accomplish, to seek after. We have to overtake our purpose—to capture it. Whatever it takes to obtain or accomplish our purpose in God, we must be willing to do it. God is looking for people that are willing to step outside the norm and follow after Him in pursuit of destiny. Understand that we do not have to settle for being mediocre. We don't serve a mediocre God. Jesus said that we would do greater works than He did.

> ***"Verily, verily, I say unto you, He that believeth on me, the works that I do shall he do also; and greater works than these shall he do; because I go unto my Father" (John 14:12).***

How can we do greater works when we don't believe that we can and hold Him to His Word? God said prove Him at His word and He will bless you.

> ***"Bring ye all the tithes into the storehouse, that there may be meat in mine house, and prove me now herewith, saith the LORD of hosts, if I will not open you the windows of heaven, and pour you out a blessing, that there shall not be room enough to receive it" (Malachi 3:10).***

Too many saints have become comfortable and complacent when it comes to pursuit of their destiny. We rely on others to pray for us as though we were not called to intercede. The devil is a liar. Religion has made us lazy. We depend on others to pray for us, to tell us what our next move is, to tell us what God is saying, to tell us what the word of God is saying, and wonder why we are stuck. As a matter of fact, I remember years ago, I was actually up in my closet, praying. The Spirit of the Lord came in so mightily that I literally flew out of my closet. He said to me that two spirits would cause many of His people to miss the mark: the spirit of religion and the spirit of unbelief. He said as far as the spirit of religion goes, many people profess Him but do not live a life of righteousness; and as far as the spirit of unbelief goes, many people believe that He created the earth. but that is as far as their belief go. Many do not believe that Jesus was born of a virgin, was God in the flesh, died for the remissions of our sins, and rose three days later with all power in His hand. In other words, many people do not believe with their hearts, which is the means by which we are saved.

> ***"That if thou shalt confess with thy mouth the Lord Jesus, and shalt believe in thine heart that God hath raised him from the dead, thou shalt be saved. 10For with the heart man believeth unto righteousness; and with the mouth confession is made unto salvation" (Romans 10:9–10).***

However, because many are called and few are chosen, as stated earlier, some have to be pushed into position. Unfortunately, when you have to be pushed, the trials can be greater.

To *push* is to press against with force in order to drive or impel, to thrust forward, to cause to increase, to press or urge forward to completion or advancement.

Hannah was pushed into position to give birth to one of the greatest prophets of the nation when her adversary provoked her yearly. However, through her pain, she reached a place in God that she probably would have never reached, if she had not been pushed.

> ***"And her adversary also provoked her sore, for to make her fret, because the LORD had shut up her womb. And as he did so year by year, when she went up to the house of the LORD, so she provoked her; therefore she wept, and did not eat" (1 Samuel 1:6–7).***

God granted her petition. She conceived and gave birth to Samuel.

Esther was pushed into position to deliver the nation of Israel after she realized what her purpose was. She realized that it wasn't a coincidence that Queen Vashti disobeyed the orders of the king and lost her position. After her uncle Modecai explained it, she realized that she was pushed into her position as queen of Babylon, by divine purpose, to help deliver God's people.

> ***For if thou altogether holdest thy peace at this time, then shall there enlargement and deliverance arise to the Jews from another place; but***

> ***thou and thy father's house shall be destroyed: and who knoweth whether thou art come to the kingdom for such a time as this? Then Esther bade them return Mordecai this answer, Go, gather together all the Jews that are present in Shushan, and fast ye for me, and neither eat nor drink three days, night or day: I also and my maidens will fast likewise; and so will I go in unto the king, which is not according to the law: and if I perish, I perish. (Esther 4:14–16)***

Esther stepped into purpose, and God used her in a mighty way. This is how He desires to use you and me. We must learn to trust Him and walk in obedience and humility. Yes, humility. God can't get the fullness of glory out of your life if you operate in a proud spirit because you will set yourself up for a fall. Pride is a dangerous thing, especially in the body of Christ. We have seen many anointed pastors and preachers fall, and oftentimes, it is because they do not walk in humility.

> ***"Pride goeth before destruction, and an haughty spirit before a fall" (Proverbs 16:18).***

Each year, the enemy unleashes thousands of spirits and forces into the atmosphere. This is why we continually hear of things that were once unheard of. That's why there're so many killings, so many suicides and murder-suicides, so many divorces—even in the body of Christ, so many pedophiles and rapes, and so much poverty. I can go on and on; however, when God is in the plan, there isn't a devil in hell that can stop you from fulfilling your purpose and walking in destiny.

Purpose is the reason you exist. It is the object toward which one strives or tries to reach. It is a result or effect that is intended for you. My purpose is to expose the enemy. His plot is to stop us from fulfilling God's plan and our destiny. He uses many devices to cause us to lose focus and get offtrack and to never come into the realization of God's divine plan and purpose for our life. Many graves are filled with individuals that missed the mark of God, never fulfilling God's intended purpose for their life. Jesus understands what it is that we have to endure for His glory to be revealed in us. He is merciful and there when we need Him. The Bible tells us that He was tempted on every hand, yet He was without sin.

> ***"For we have not an high priest which cannot be touched with the feeling of our infirmities;***

> ***but was in all points tempted like as we are, yet without sin. Let us therefore come boldly unto the throne of grace, that we may obtain mercy, and find grace to help in time of need" (Hebrews 4:15–16).***

Jesus's sacrifice was the ultimate display of love and glory.

> ***Let this mind be in you, which was also in Christ Jesus: Who, being in the form of God, thought it not robbery to be equal with God: But made himself of no reputation, and took upon him the form of a servant, and was made in the likeness of men: And being found in fashion as a man, he humbled himself, and became obedient unto death, even the death of the cross. Wherefore, God also hath highly exalted him, and given him a name which is above every name: That at the name of Jesus every knee should bow, of things in heaven, and things in earth, and things under the earth; And that every tongue should confess that Jesus***

> ***Christ is Lord, to the glory of God the Father. (Philippians 2:5–11)***

Just as Jesus was created for God's glory, so were we. God made us for Him. He desires for us to declare His name and be a witness for Him throughout the earth and to every generation. His original plan was to rule earth from heaven through man.

> ***Jesus, when he had cried again with a loud voice, yielded up the ghost. And, behold, the veil of the temple was rent in twain from the top to the bottom; and the earth did quake, and the rocks rent; And the graves were opened; and many bodies of the saints which slept arose, And came out of the graves after his resurrection, and went into the holy city, and appeared unto many. (Matthew 27:50–53)***

His sacrifice not only gave us life but also gave us free access to God. We can communicate with God anytime we want, or need, to. God hears a broken and contrite spirit, as I mentioned before. We can seek Him for guidance and direction. When the graves of the saints were opened, at Jesus's resurrection, so were ours. We now have the right to the tree of life. We can live and fulfill God's divine plan for our life. I thank God that on that night that I prayed and cried out to Him, He inclined His ear unto me and answered. That was the day that I chose *life*!

CPSIA information can be obtained
at www.ICGtesting.com
Printed in the USA
LVHW041913051119
636471LV00001B/1